Introduction to Coding

for Class VI

A perfect textbook to learn Basics of Block Coding through Activities and Projects

S P Verma
M.Sc., M.Ed., PGCPM
Former Principal, KVS, New Delhi

www.bpbonline.com

FIRST EDITION 2022

ISBN: 978-93-5551-176-8

Distributors:

BPB PUBLICATIONS
20, Ansari Road, Darya Ganj
New Delhi-110002
Ph: 23254990/23254991

DECCAN AGENCIES
4-3-329, Bank Street,
Hyderabad-500195
Ph: 24756967/24756400

MICRO MEDIA
Shop No. 5, Mahendra Chambers,
150 DN Rd. Next to Capital Cinema,
V.T. (C.S.T.) Station, MUMBAI-400 001
Ph: 22078296/22078297

BPB BOOK CENTRE
376 Old Lajpat Rai Market,
Delhi-110006
Ph: 23861747

Published by Manish Jain for BPB Publications, 20 Ansari Road, Darya Ganj, New Delhi-110002 and Printed by him at Manipal Technologies Limited, Manipal

www.bpbonline.com

Dedicated to

My Grand-Parents
(Late Mr Nyadar Singh Verma & Mrs. Chawali Devi)

My Parents
(Late Dr. Shiv Swaroop Verma & Mrs. Swaroopi Verma)

My Grandson
(Dearest Atharv Verma)

and

All Lovely Learners

About the Author

S P Verma, M.Sc; M.Ed; PGCPM has been working in the field of education since last 35 years. As a seasoned educationist, teacher trainer, career counsellor, academic auditor, motivator, mentor, author and editor, he has authored 55 school books, 6 research papers, 10 research articles, more than 70 articles on careers and edited more than 200 educational products. More than 20k educators (teachers and principals) attended his training sessions across the country. More than 200k students were career counselled and inspired to take right career plan by him.

Formerly holding the positions as Principal, Kendriya Vidyalaya Sangathan, New Delhi; Regional Director, Teacher Sity, New Delhi; Regional Director, iDC, New Delhi; and Director (School Trg), Vidya Institute of Training and Development, VKP, Meerut; he is now associated as Director (Trg and Innovation) with GEM Foundations, Bengaluru. Besides Associate Life Member of Computer Society of India (CSI), he is associated with a number of professional bodies as Life Member, like Vigyan Parishad, Allahabad; Hindi Vigyan Sahitya Parishad, BARC, Mumbai; InSc, Bengaluru, PTAI, New Delhi, etc.

Acknowledgements

I would like to acknowledge the contributions of all the educationists (teachers and principals), professionals, and reviewers, who provided their feedback and suggestions on the MS of this book. Especially, I am grateful to **Mr. Pavnesh Kumar**, Former Controller of Examinations, CBSE; **Dr DK Sharma**, Dean (School of Engineering and Technolgy), IIMT University, Meerut; **Prof. RC Singh**, Controller of Examinations, Sharda University, Greater Noida; **Mr. Akshay Sharma**, B.Tech., ONGC, Mehsana, **Mr Shubham Verma**, B.Tech., MBA and **Mrs. Shweta Agrawal**, MCA for their specific suggestions.

It's my proud privilege to put on record my sincere gratitude to my publisher **M/s BPB Publications**, New Delhi, for accepting my vision and plan of writing Coding books for classes VI to VIII and providing me the opportunity for the same. The initial interaction with **Mr. Manish Jain**, CEO, and **Mr. Varun Jain**, Director was fruitful in making a long-term association and bonding. I am grateful to them and the entire team of BPB Publications for bringing out these publications in a short span of time.

I am grateful to my well-wishers namely **Mr. RL Jamuda**, Former Commissioner KVS; **Dr. MM Swami**, Former Deputy Commisioner, KVS; **Mr VK Gupta**, Former Deputy Commissioner, KVS; **Mr. DK Saini**, Former Deputy Commissioner, KVS; **Mr AK Verma**, CEO, Eduwix, New Delhi; **Mr NK Verma**, AGM, BHEL HQ; **Mr AK Pattnaik**, SrGM (Academic), Kalorex Group of Institutions, Ahmedabad; **Mr YP Sharma**, **Mr Vipin Agrawal**; **Mr. Matin Ahmed**, **Mr. NK Giri**, **Mr NK Bansal** and **Mr SC Sharma** for their constant support, help and motivation to do something good to the society.

I am touched by the love, patience and tolerance shown, during the completion of this project, by my family members- **Mrs. Rekha Verma** (Life Partner), **Sqn Ldr Anuj Verma** (Son), Dearest **Atharv** (Grandson) and **Mrs. Shelja Sharma**, B.Tech., B.Ed., MBA (Daughter in Law). I am grateful to them as well as to all my friends and relatives supporting me in all the creative tasks.

While preparing the manuscript of this book, I have gone through a number of books and different websites. I am grateful to all those authors, contributors, editors, freelancers whose articles are read and used in one or another way in this book. And last but not least, I am indebted to God for keeping my brain alive and my health sound even at the time of the Covid Pandemic so that He could get completed this task through me.

— S P Verma

Preface

It gives me immense pleasure to put the first edition of **"Introduction to Coding (for class VI)"** before the enthusiastic learners. Coding and Artificial intelligence is getting more attention in the world day by day. Coding is touching almost all fields related to the development of the human-beings. AI based Technology using coding and it applications is changing at a very fast rate influencing day-to-day life positively. AI and coding are nowadays applied in almost all fields, be it education, transport management, air traffic control, medicine manufacturing, space research, customer care, pandemic control, or entertainment.

After understanding the importance and demand of Coding and AI, the Govt of India, through CBSE, has launched Skills Development subjects from class VI onwards, including Coding, Artificial Intelligence, etc. CBSE has introduced 'Coding' as a skill module of 12 hours duration in classes VI-VIII from the Session 2021-2022 onwards to simplify the coding learning experience. It is an attempt to nurture design thinking, logical flow of ideas and apply this across the disciplines.

This book is written according to the latest guidelines and syllabus of Coding issued by CBSE. The main objective of writing this series of books for classes VI to VIII is to provide technical knowledge with all practical aspects of Block Coding without the use of any programming language, like Python. Thus, the learners will become fully competent to face the challenges of living in an AI-based applications-equipped futuristic society. Moreover, emphasis on the development of 21st Century Life Skills through a variety of activities, practical and projects is laid down.

The book contains five chapters and two annexures. The salient features of the book are as follows:

- Its content is written after following the guidelines provided by CBSE.
- It explains the concepts of Coding with proper examples in lucid language.
- Simple, easy, and understandable language is used to clarify the content.
- It incorporates a pictorial setup in presenting the content by using tables, charts, graphs, pictures, photographs, etc.
- It illustrates a good number of **'Solved Examples on Block Coding'**.
- **Activities and Projects** have been incorporated for inculcating 21St Century Life Skills, including creativity, innovation, critical thinking, team work, working in a diverse environment, etc.
- Important concepts are provided as ***'Summary'*** at the end of each chapter.
- **'Coding Quiz'** section provide an opportunity for learners to test their knowledge in a fun way.
- **'Practice Time'** section contains all sorts of questions including HOTS.
- **'Factz Funda'** provides additional information related to the content of the chapter.
- **Some Unsolved Projects** are provided at the end of chapter to practice the concepts learned in the chapter.
- Two Annexures providing extra useful information are annexed at the end of the book.

I am sure that the sincere efforts put in by the author and publication team will be well received by the dynamic, dedicated and passionate teachers, and energetic learners. The author will appreciate all sorts of feedback from the readers to improve the quality of the content.

SP Verma

Email: spv1962@gmail.com

Coloured Images

Please follow the link to download the
Coloured Images of the book:

https://rebrand.ly/2ukn1sf

We have code bundles from our rich catalogue of books and videos available at **https://github.com/bpbpublications**. Check them out!

Errata

We take immense pride in our work at BPB Publications and follow best practices to ensure the accuracy of our content to provide with an indulging reading experience to our subscribers. Our readers are our mirrors, and we use their inputs to reflect and improve upon human errors, if any, that may have occurred during the publishing processes involved. To let us maintain the quality and help us reach out to any readers who might be having difficulties due to any unforeseen errors, please write to us at :

errata@bpbonline.com

Your support, suggestions and feedbacks are highly appreciated by the BPB Publications' Family.

Piracy

If you come across any illegal copies of our works in any form on the internet, we would be grateful if you would provide us with the location address or website name. Please contact us at **business@bpbonline.com** with a link to the material.

If you are interested in becoming an author

If there is a topic that you have expertise in, and you are interested in either writing or contributing to a book, please visit **www.bpbonline.com**. We have worked with thousands of developers and tech professionals, just like you, to help them share their insights with the global tech community. You can make a general application, apply for a specific hot topic that we are recruiting an author for, or submit your own idea.

Reviews

Please leave a review. Once you have read and used this book, why not leave a review on the site that you purchased it from? Potential readers can then see and use your unbiased opinion to make purchase decisions. We at BPB can understand what you think about our products, and our authors can see your feedback on their book. Thank you!

For more information about BPB, please visit **www.bpbonline.com**.

Table of Contents

Ethical Approach in Coding

All the teachers and learners who have to build capabilities around coding, will be equipped, through the course on coding, to build software on your own. This will have an impact on society in general. Hence, it is crucial to follow ethical practices while building your own code.

Some ethical practices given as below are to be followed while learning to code:

- Contribute to society and human wellbeing.
- Limit negative results of software, including dangers to safety, health, personal security, and privacy.
- Limit the aftereffects of the software.
- Ensure your Code respects diversity and is utilized responsibly with social issues in mind.
- Promote environmental sustainability both locally and globally.
- Avoid harm to others.
- Avoid to become the cause of physical or mental injury, unjustified destruction to property or information.
- Avoid unjustified damage to environment.

Introduction to Coding

Structure

In this chapter, you will learn:

- Real-world application of coding
- Impacts of coding in our daily lives
- Meaning of coding in the context of computer science

INTRODUCTION

We live in a tech-savvy world where people are using a large number of machines in their daily lives. Various machines are used for different types of work. You can just see around in your house how many machines are used for different tasks, like washing clothes, mopping the floor, for entertainment, for communication, transportation, traffic control, etc. Some machines are programmed to do some specific functions with the help of in-built computers. Whereas some machines (smart machines) perform the tasks with perfection without being tired. Many machines are fitted with coding/programs to perform tasks and to learn new things over time.

In this chapter, we will learn about coding and its applications in daily life.

Figure 1.1

Learning Objectives:

At the end of this chapter, you will be able to:

- Understand how coding is being used in everyday life to perform complex tasks in an easy manner.
- Understand the real-life applications of coding.
- Understand exactly the meaning of the term coding in the context of computer science.
- Know the names of some of the most popular programming languages.

1.1 HOW DO TRAFFIC LIGHTS WORK?

You must have seen the use of traffic lights/signals fitted at the busy crossing on roads. But have you ever wondered how traffic signals function to control traffic? Normally, in almost all countries, three lights -Green, Yellow and Red, are used as traffic signals. The lights cycle goes through green, yellow, and red at a regular interval to control road intersections' traffic flow. The traffic signals prevent accidents and help to avoid congestion on the roads. It is interesting to know how the traffic lights change automatically. Few lines of code/program running in the background drive the traffic lights/signals. At regular intervals, the code/program changes the traffic signals to run lights of different colours. With the help of sensors, sometimes it functions even smarter; when the code detects congestion on a particular road, then it maximizes the time of traffic flow in a particular direction to reduce the traffic load on the road. Sometimes, code allows the functioning when traffic is present on the road/crossings.

Figure 1.2: Traffic lights

Factz Funda

Lester Wire (from the USA) invented the first electric traffic light in 1912 that had two signals- red and green. However, this invention was never patented.

1.2 APPLICATIONS OF CODING

Most humans knowingly or unknowingly engage with coding/programming in some devices, be it inside our homes or outside. The use of coding can be seen in almost all areas/places, like on the streets, at the schools, at a shopping complex, in a mall, at the local grocery stores, etc. Some practical examples of usage of coding are enlisted in Table 1.1.

Activity 1.1

- Participate in the larger group activity on "Applications of coding in daily life."
- The teacher will initiate the class discussion on the topic by giving few examples and will motivate the students to share their views in open house discussions.
- One student will note down the responses from all the students and will prepare the list of applications of coding in daily life.
- He/she will put the prepared list before the full class after the discussion.

Table 1.1 Some of the practical examples where coding is used

- Interaction with bar-code scanners at shopping store
- Automatic control of traffic using traffic lights
- Booking movie,
- Automated vacuum cleaner
- Automatic washing machine
- Automatic toys
- Booking of bus, train, flight tickets online
- 3D Printers
- Computer software like a web browser
- Video games
- Animations for entertainment
- TV remote
- AC remote
- Drone
- Casio music keyboard
- Musical birthday/greeting card
- Credit card/Debit card with Chip & PIN (Personal Identification Number) to perform a specific task or achieve a particular result.

Factz Funda

Traffic Light Information System is a system by which the driver could know at which speed he/she needs to drive in order to pass the green light.

1.3 WHAT IS CODING ACTUALLY?

The process of creating instructions that can be executed on a computer to solve a problem is called coding/programming. Coding is similar to solve a math problem. There may be many ways to solve a problem. In the same way, there could be more than one method to write code/program for the same problem/ task.

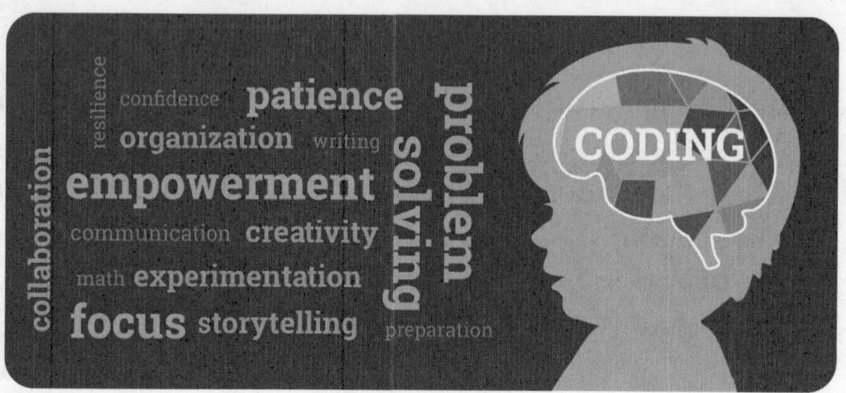

Figure 1.3

We use different methods for solving a problem. Similarly, some coding approaches are more efficient than others while dealing with a particular problem. Consider this situation: you are playing a video game on your smartphone. Because your smartphone is like a computer, hence it needs to be instructed on what to be done. The app playing the video game provides the instruction(s). The video-playing app is an example of coding/ programming. But the interesting question is how the app communicates the instructions to the phone. Actually, it does through a coding/programming language. We will learn more about programming languages in this chapter too.

Factz Funda

Spacewar was the first computer game, and it was created by MIT programmer Steve Russel and his team in 1961.

Figure 1.4: Spacewar

1.4 PROGRAMMING LANGUAGE

When someone wants to convey a message to another person (s), what does he do? Think about how many ways we communicate with people around us? Humans use language as primary means of communication for all interactions or communications. On the same lines, humans can interact with computers through a language that computers can understand. Computers do not understand the languages spoken by human beings. This type of language is called a coding/ programming language. Humans can provide instructions to a computer to perform a set of activities by using programming/coding language. The person who uses a programming language to write a code/program for solving a particular problem is called a coder/programmer. The sets of instructions are also called programs. As different languages have grammar rules to understand and use that language, programming languages also have syntax. Thus, the syntax is a set of rules that coders need to follow when they write a computer program.

Figure 1.5: Programming languages

Coders use many programming languages around the world, and new ones are getting developed all the time. Whereas each programming language has its own syntax, but all programming languages have one thing in common, i.e., they are eventually converted into a language that the computer will understand. In this and the following chapters, we will learn about different programming techniques and how to apply them in solving various problems. Some of the most frequently used programming languages are given in Table 1.2.

Factz Funda

Coders are using more than 700 programming languages for writing codes throughout the world, and this number is increasing.

Table 1.2 Most frequently used programming languages.

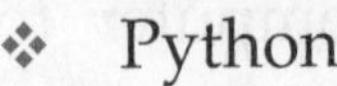

- Python
- Java
- JavaScript
- Lua
- C
- COBOL
- C++
- Scratch
- C#
- R
- F#

Factz Funda

A smartphone runs on more code than NASA's computers in 1969. This clearly means that the code that sent the man to space was less complex as compared to the code that runs the smartphone.

1.5 YOUNG CODERS FROM INDIA

(*i*) Six-year-old **Raja Anirudh Sri Ram** from Tirupati has become the youngest child in India to be certified as **'Microsoft Office Specialist,'** setting a new record and entering 'India Book of Records'. Anirudh secured this distinction mark by scoring 914 marks in his second attempt on August 21, 2021.

Anirudh, who is a student of Class 2 at Edify School, aspires to become an astronaut in the future. As a rule, 700 marks out of 1000 are considered as pass marks for the certification. He could not clear the exam in his first attempt on 14 Aug. 2021. However, he cleared it in his second attempt with a record 914 marks.

Figure 1.6: Raja Anirudh Sri Ram with 'Microsoft Office Specialist' certificate (Reference: Indian Express September 05, 2021)

(*ii*) **Arham Om Talsania** is just six years old, and he recently made it to the Guinness Book of World Records as the world's youngest computer programmer. The class 2nd student from Ahmedabad, Gujarat, has cleared the Microsoft certification exam at Pearson Vue Test Centre.

Figure 1.7: Arham Om Talsania

(*iii*) **Hirranya Rajani**, six years old and a student of Oberoi International School, Goregaon, Mumbai, has developed a sign language app for hearing impaired people.

Figure 1.8: Hirranya Rajani

1.6 IMPACT OF CODING IN OUR LIVES

Coding is affecting our lives positively because we are using a large number of machines and apps based on codes to make our lives easier and comfortable. Coding is turning into an inevitable task for students. Coding is just like writing an essay with the help of essay samples. During the coding/programming process, various life skills are developed among the students. When the students are involved in coding, they actually learn how to solve a problem by using their analytical skills, creativity, communication skills, and computational skills.

Ability is the capacity to do some work, like the ability to read, write, measure, think, etc. A person has more than 90 abilities. A skill is the ability to perform a task with perfection. Thus, a skill is achieved by practicing an ability. The Ministry of Education in India has even started to include coding/programming as a core curriculum in schools. Life skills developed during coding are given in Table 1.3.

Table 1.3 List of Lifeskills improved during coding

- Critical thinking skills
- Problem-solving skill,
- Computational thinking,
- Leadership-related skills.
- Analytical thinking,
- Creative thinking,
- Empathy
- Team building skill

Coding is impacting human lives to a great extent. It will continue to be an integral part of our lives in the future too. Moreover, the addition of technology to traditional classrooms has a positive impact on the minds of young learners. And coding helps to understand technology better and grow in close adaptation to it. Coding will open new avenues for the present generations, and it will inbuild the attributes of problem-solving skills, creativity, logical thinking, persistence, and other cognitive abilities.

Figure 1.9

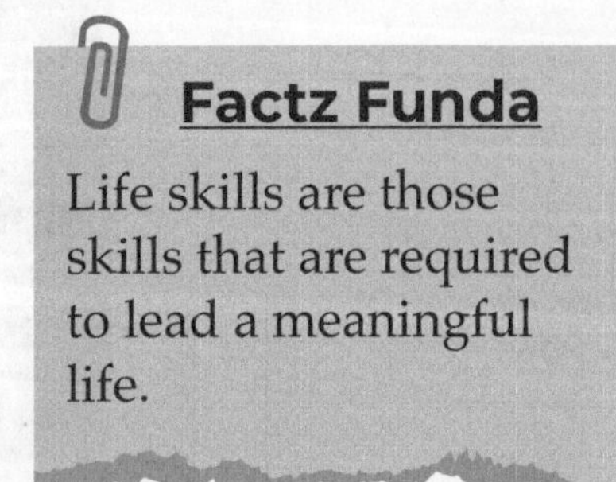

Moreover, coders are in heavy demand nowadays. It opens up a whole new world of possibilities for people today. When you are equipped with the ability to code, it only means that you are 'digitally updated/ at par' with the era of coding and programming. After getting skilled in coding, one can have many job roles, like web developers, mobile app developers, full-stack developers, system engineers, database administrators, etc.

Coding Quiz

1. OTP and Pin authentication for ATM card transactions is an example of programming.

   (a) True (b) False

2. For any specific problem, there is always only one method to write a program.

   (a) True (b) False

3. Consider this statement: 'Code is a set of instructions that can be executed on a computer to perform a specific task.' The statement is:

   (a) True (b) False

4. Which example(s) is/are related to programming in real life?

   (a) Robots (b) Computer Games

   (c) Self-drive cars (d) All the above

5. Which language is not an example of a programming language?

   (a) Python (b) French

   (c) JavaScript (d) C++

6. Which of the following pairs is an example of programming language?

   (a) Python, Java (b) C++, Lua

   (c) JavaScript, Scratch (d) All the above

ANSWERS
1. (a) 2. (b) 3. (a) 4. (d) 5. (b) 6. (d)

SUMMARY

- Coding is used in many devices used by humans to make life comfortable.
- The process of creating instructions that can be executed on a computer to solve a problem is called coding/programming.
- Coding is impacting human lives to a large extent in a positive way.
- Coding helps in developing many life skills among learners.
- The traffic signals prevent accidents and help to avoid congestion on the roads.
- The traffic lights change automatically.
- Few lines of code/program running in the background drive the traffic lights/signals.

- Lester Wire (from the USA) invented the first electric traffic light in 1912 that had two signals- red and green.
- Interaction with bar-code scanners at shopping store use coding.
- Traffic Light Information System is a system by which the driver could know at which speed he/she needs to drive in order to pass the green light.
- The process of creating instructions that can be executed on a computer to solve a problem is called coding/programming.
- Some coding approaches are more efficient than others while dealing with a particular problem.
- Spacewar was the first computer game,that was created by MIT programmer Steve Russel and his team in 1961.
- Computers do not understand the languages called coding/programming language.
- The person who uses a programming language to write a code/program for solving a particular problem is called a coder/programmer.
- The sets of instructions framed by coder are also called programs.
- The syntax is a set of rules that coders need to follow when they write a computer program.
- Most frequently used programming languages include Python, C++ , Java, Scratch, JavaScript, Lua, R, COBOL, etc.
- Coding is affecting our lives positively because we are using a large number of machines and apps based on codes to make our lives easier and comfortable.

PRACTICE TIME

(A) True/False Type Questions

1. Coding is also known as programming.
2. Coder is a person who writes the program to solve a given problem.
3. A problem can have the only one solution.
4. Code is a set of instructions that a computer can understand to execute a particular task.
5. Programming language can be understood by humans but not by computers.
6. Python is a popular programming language.
7. The process of creating instructions that can be executed on a computer to solve a problem is called coding/programming.
8. The traffic lights change manually.

9. The traffic signals prevent accidents and help to avoid congestion on the roads.
10. The sets of instructions framed by coder are also called programs.

ANSWERS							
1. T	2. T	3. F	4. T	5. F	6. T	7. T	8. F (automatically)
9. T	10. T						

(B) Fill in the Blanks

1. ____________ is used in many devices used by humans to make life comfortable.
2. ____________ (from the USA) invented the first electric traffic light in 1912 that had two signals- red and green.
3. ____________ was the first computer game,that was created by MIT programmer Steve Russel and his team in 1961.
4. The person who uses a programming language to write a code/program for solving a particular problem is called a ____________.
5. Coding is impacting human lives to a large extent in a ____________ way.
6. Coding helps in developing many ____________ skills among learners.
7. The ____________ is a set of rules that coders need to follow when they write a computer program.
8. The process of creating instructions that can be executed on a computer to solve a problem is called ____________.
9. Some coding approaches are more ____________ than others while dealing with a particular problem.
10. Python, C++, Java, Scratch, JavaScript, Lua, R, COBOL, etc. are the examples of ____________.

ANSWERS			
1. Coding	2. Lester Wire	3. Spacewar	4. coder
5. positive	6. life	7. syntax	8. coding/programming.
9. efficient	10. programming languages		

(C) Very Short Answers Questions

1. What is coding?
2. Define programming language.
3. What do you mean by a coder?

4. Can computers understand the languages spoken by humans?
5. What is the common feature of all programming languages?

(D) Short Answer Questions

1. Give three examples of programming languages.
2. Why is a programming language required?
3. Give three examples where coding is used.

(E) High Order Thinking Skill Questions (HOTS)

1. What will happen if there is no traffic light in a big city like New Delhi or Mumbai?
2. How is coding affecting human life?

2 Algorithms with Block Coding

Structure

In this chapter, you will learn:

- The meaning of the term algorithm.
- About a flowchart.
- Applications of Flowchart.
- The meaning of pseudocode.
- The usage of block coding through the MakeCode platform.

INTRODUCTION

Coding is behind almost every machine that is powered by electricity. Coding is sometimes called the "language of the future" as it has become the inevitable truth of the future. The learners are required to learn how to communicate properly with technology. Coding is used now in creating and building technology from scratch. It is crucial to introduce coding to a child from an early age to develop a key interest in the language of technology. This is because it enhances the cognitive abilities of a child by developing the creative and problem-solving skills in them. Also, this helps in ensuring logical decision-making in a child.

In this chapter, we shall learn about the algorithm, flow chart, and their applications.

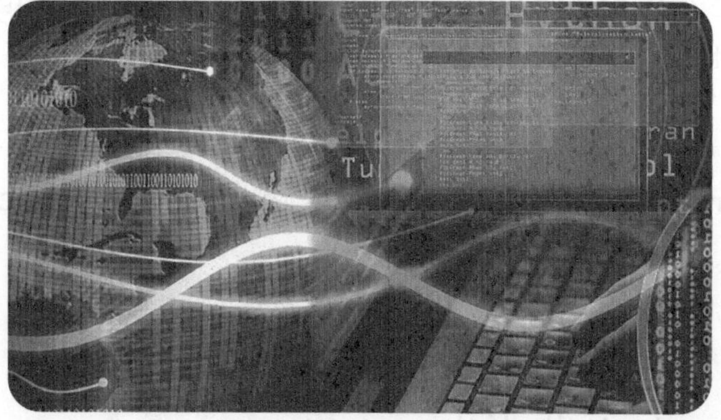

Figure 2.1

Learning Objectives:

At the end of this chapter, you will be able to:

- have a basic understanding of algorithms, flowchart, and pseudocode.
- Have practiced following a step-by-step approach to solving a problem using block-based programming.
- Get oriented to the MakeCode platform.

2.1 DEFINING PROGRAM

A set of instructions to perform a specific task when executed by a computer is called a program. It is usually written in a specific programming language, like Python. Software development requires many tasks to be incorporated to follow an organized plan and a series of sub-tasks in a well-defined chronological order. The ABCD Rule is followed to better understand the intermediate steps of a computer program before documentation.

(i) Analysing the problem:

- Read and understand the basic functionalities of the problem carefully.
- List the inputs required.
- List the required calculations to get the desired output.

(ii) Broadcasting the developed algorithm:

- Plan all the actions required and their sequence before writing a program.
- Use the English language to write a program.

(iii) Coding the program:

- Convert the plan into the algorithm that is understood by the computer.
- Use a language out of available many programming languages, like C, C++, Java, Python, etc.

(iv) Testing and debugging the program

- Test the program by giving various inputs and check the outputs for correctness.
- Analyze the syntax errors, if any (No output in case of syntax error in the program)
- Correct the errors logically if the outputs are incorrect.

(v) Documentation of the program

Creating and maintaining the documents related to the program.

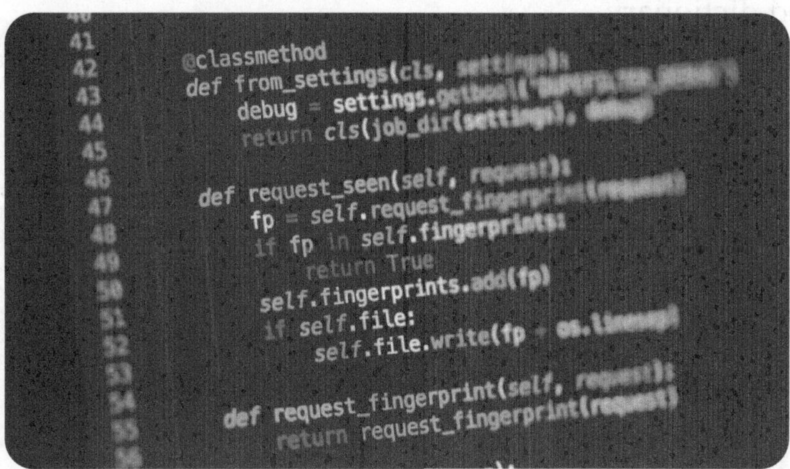

Figure 2.2: Documentation of the program

2.2 ALGORITHM

In computers, an algorithm means the process required for planning and solving the problems. A sequence of steps to solve any particular problem is called an algorithm. The word "Algorithm" is also related to the name of the mathematician Al-Khwarizmi, which means a procedure or a technique.

Activity 2.1

Searching for a word in the dictionary

- Participate in the individual activity on finding a word in the dictionary.
- Take a dictionary and search the word "Piracy" in it to find its meaning.
- What steps you will take to find out this word in the dictionary. Think and write.

____

____

____

____

____

____

- Now, search out the word and write its meaning here:

____

Check whether you have followed the following set of steps to search out the given word "Piracy" in the dictionary:

- Take a good dictionary.
- First, find the dictionary section with the first letter of the word, i.e., 'P.'
- Then, within the list of words starting the second letter 'i'.
- Then, find the section having the third letter of the word 'r.'
- Repeat the process with the fourth, fifth, and sixth letters until to reach the word 'piracy' in the dictionary.
- And then find its meaning.

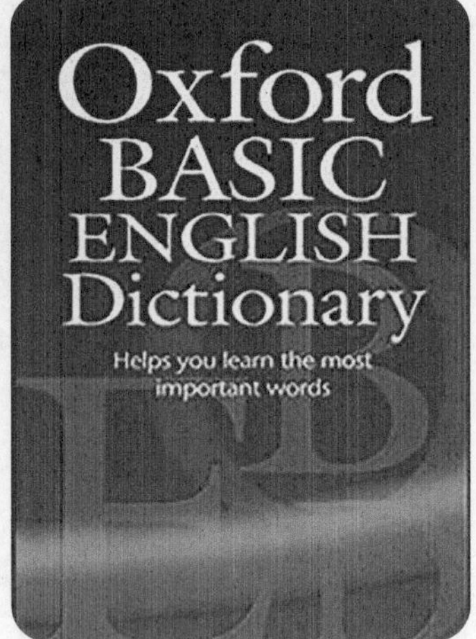

Figure 2.3

Thus, it can be understood now that before writing a program code for a given problem in computer science, it is essential to devise a set of steps to be followed to solve the problem. This type of set of steps is called an algorithm. Therefore, in computer science, 'an algorithm is defined as the step-by-step plan to solve the problem for a given problem statement.'

Factz Funda

The first programming language was Fortran (FORmula TRANslation) that was created by John Backus and his team at IBM in the 1950s.

2.2.1 Steps to Write Algorithms

Step 1: Define the inputs for the algorithm: Define the inputs required for the algorithm. Various algorithms take in data for processing. For example, while calculating the circumference of a circle, input will be the radius.

Step 2: Define the variables: Variables in an algorithm may be used by the user for more than one place, and hence, variables are to be defined. While calculating the circumference of a circle, we need to define radius (variable).

Step 3: Outline the algorithm's operations: Outlining the operations of the algorithm is required to input variables for computation purposes. For example, to find the circumference of a circle, multiply the value of pie (3.14) with two times radius. Thus, circumference (2* (3.14)* radius) is defined.

Step 4: Output the results of the operations of the algorithm: Outline the result(s) of the operations of the algorithm. In the case of the area of a circle, the output will be the value stored in the variable ' circumference.'

2.3 FLOWCHARTS

The solution of a problem can be shown by a diagrammatic representation of the sequence of the steps. This is called Flowchart.

2.3.1 Meaning of a Flowchart

A flowchart is a diagrammatic representation of the step-by-step plan to be followed for solving a task/ problem statement. The diagrammatic representation of the plan is made up of different geometric shapes like boxes, diamonds, parallelograms, circles, and ellipses connected by arrows. Each shape acts as a step in the solution/product/ output, and the arrows represent the direction of flow among the steps.

In other words, 'A flow chart or a flowchart is a type of diagram, made of boxes and arrows.' It can be used to show an algorithm, a process, and/ the planned stages of a period.

It is better to understand the terms as follows:

- ❖ An algorithm is a list of step-by-step list of directions required to be followed to solve a problem.
- ❖ A process is a series of stages in time when the last stage is the product, result, or goal.
- ❖ The planned stages of a period.

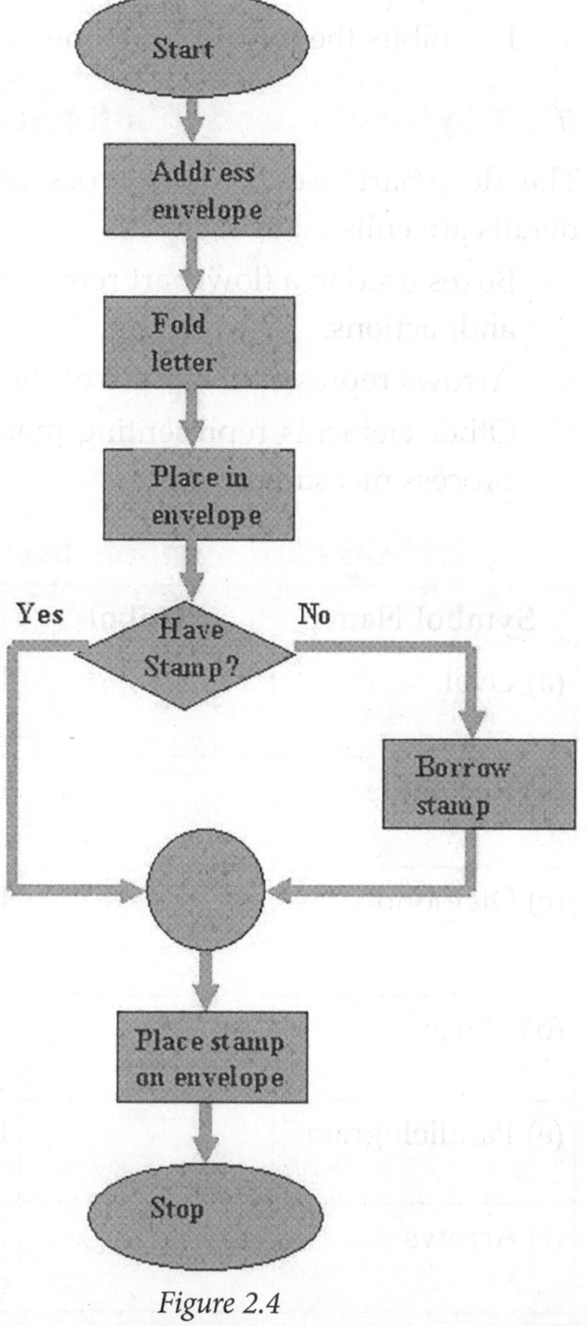

Figure 2.4

2.3.2 Characteristics of a Flowchart

- It represents a workflow or process in a diagrammatic representation.
- It consists of standardized symbols.
- It exhibits the sequence of instructions/happenings in a single program.
- It shows the logic of an algorithm from start to end.
- It has short, clear, and readable statements written inside the symbols.
- It should have a clear start point and Endpoint.
- It shows the individual steps and their interconnections.
- It exhibits the control from one activity to the next one.

2.3.3 Symbols used in a flowchart

The flowchart uses various types of boxes, arrows, and other elements. The details are enlisted in Table 2.1.

- Boxes used in a flowchart represent the process operations, the various steps, and/ actions.
- Arrows represent the order of the steps and/or different options.
- Other elements representing materials involved, decisions, people, time, or process measurements.

Table 2.1 Standard symbols used in the flowchart

Symbol Name	Symbol	Function
(a) Oval		It is used to show the start and the end of program in flowchart.
(b) Rectangle		It is used to show processing for arithmetic operations and data-manipulations.
(c) Diamond		It is used to represent the operation in which there are two/three alternatives.
(d) Circle		It is used as page connector.
(e) Parallelogram		It is used for input and output operation.
(f) Arrows		Arrows are used to indicate the direction of flow of sequence by connecting symbols.

2.3.4 Benefits of using a flowchart

Some of the benefits of using a flowchart are given below:

- The flow chart shows the logic of a program in a simple way.
- It helps to explain the approach to solving a problem.
- It is easy and efficient to analyze the problem using a flow chart.
- It helps in practical problem-solving.
- The flow chart makes program or system maintenance easier.
- It is easy to convert the flow chart into any programming language code.
- The Flowchart helps in bringing in visual clarity to a problem.
- Once a flowchart is prepared, it remains as documentation of the code and can be used to understand the code as and when required.

Factz Funda

Herman Goldstine and John von Neumann developed flowcharts first time in the 1940s.

Activity 2.2

- Participate in the individual activity on **"Making a flow chart on profit and loss."**
- Prepare a flowchart on profit or loss by taking two inputs, i.e., cost price (CP) and selling price (SP).
- Then, calculate profit or loss depending on the values of CP and SP and print the same.
- The Flowchart will look as given here:

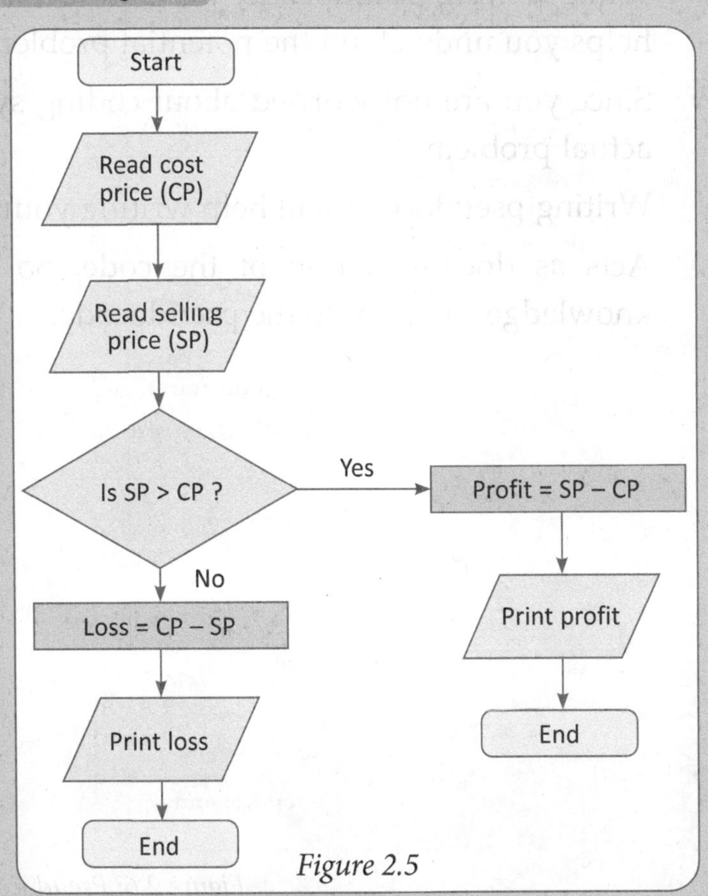

Figure 2.5

2.4 PSEUDOCODE

The pseudocode in computer science is a plain language description of all the steps of an algorithm.

2.4.1 Meaning of a Pseudocode

In computer science, pseudocode is used to describe the steps followed in an algorithm via simple human-comprehensible language. Thus, pseudocode has no syntax of any programming language and can be understood by a layman.

2.4.2 Advantages of pseudocodes

The advantages of representing the solution as pseudocode are multifield:

- ❖ The focus is mainly on including all the essential steps to solve the problem. Thus, the solution tends to be comprehensive.
- ❖ Reviewers can quickly review the pseudocode and verify if the steps will generate the desired outcome or not.
- ❖ While writing pseudocode, you can focus on all possible scenarios. So, this helps you understand the potential problems that might come up later.
- ❖ Since you are not worried about coding syntax, you can concentrate on the actual problem.
- ❖ Writing pseudocode will help writing your code in much easier language.
- ❖ Acts as documentation of the code. So even a layman with no coding knowledge can refer to the pseudocode.

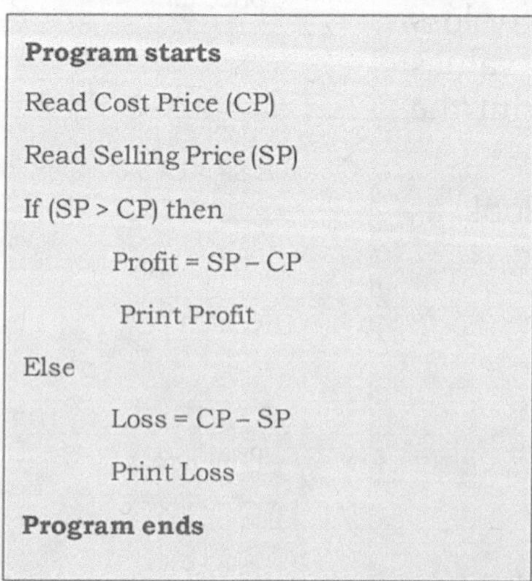

```
Program starts
Read Cost Price (CP)
Read Selling Price (SP)
If (SP > CP) then
        Profit = SP – CP
        Print Profit
Else
        Loss = CP – SP
        Print Loss
Program ends
```

Figure 2.6: Pseudocode

Activity 2.3

- Participate in the individual activity on **'Profit and loss with pseudocode.'**
- Prepare pseudocode of Profit and loss activity. Here, you have to write the program which can be understood by even a layman.
- The pseudocode is shown below:

```
Program starts
Read Cost Price (CP)
Read Selling Price (SP)
If (SP > CP) then
     Profit = SP - CP
     Print Profit
Else
     Loss = CP - SP
     Print Loss
Program ends
```

2.5 BLOCK CODING

Block coding is a type of visual programming that represents code as blocks on a graphical interface. It is opposite to the text-based languages associated with conventional programming. Different kinds of blocks represent various constructs found in programming languages, like conditional statements, loops, and functions. The user can rearrange these blocks using the drag-and-drop method. Program behaviour is typically customized by choosing different options from drop-down menus and filling in text boxes.

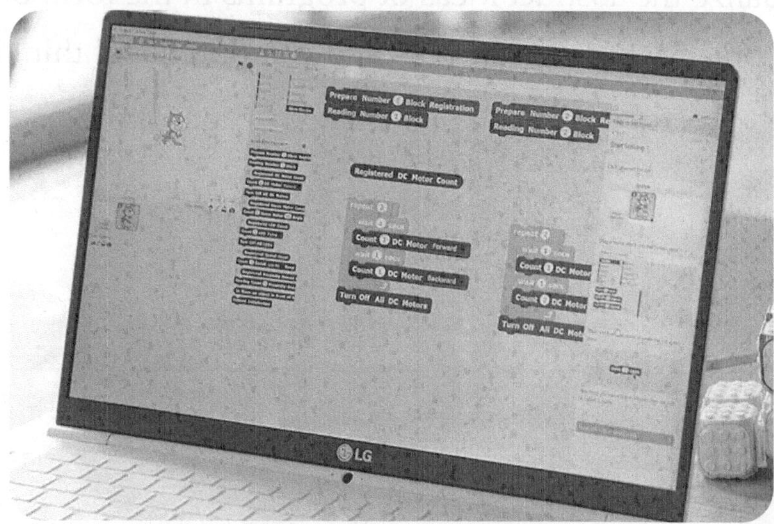

Figure 2.7: Block coding

It is rightly said that block coding is not a substitute for real (text-based) code as it has its limitations, but it bridges the gap. Thus, younger students can learn about coding sooner. The main benefit of block coding is that it clarifies the students how to give clear instructions and organize their thoughts to writing sequences. Moreover, block coding helps young students practice coding concepts and computational thinking.

While the block coding approach makes it easy to start programming, but it starts to lose its effectiveness for applications on increasing size and complexity. Dragging and dropping blocks is simply perfect for creating simple, easy-to-understand programs for combining a few programming constructs. But this doesn't scale well. When we add more functionality, the number of blocks grows rapidly, and it makes it harder to keep track of everything. Moreover, the relationships between blocks become increasingly obscured.

Factz Funda

The process of finding and fixing errors in the code is known as debugging. Many traditional programming languages have significant resources to aid the debugging process.

2.5.1 Benefits of Block Coding

- Learning block coding is easy and fun.
- It clarifies to the students how to give clear instructions.
- It helps the students in organizing their thoughts in the form of writing sequences.
- Easy to visualize the abstract ideas of programs in the form of blocks.
- It is easy to practice coding concepts and computational thinking.

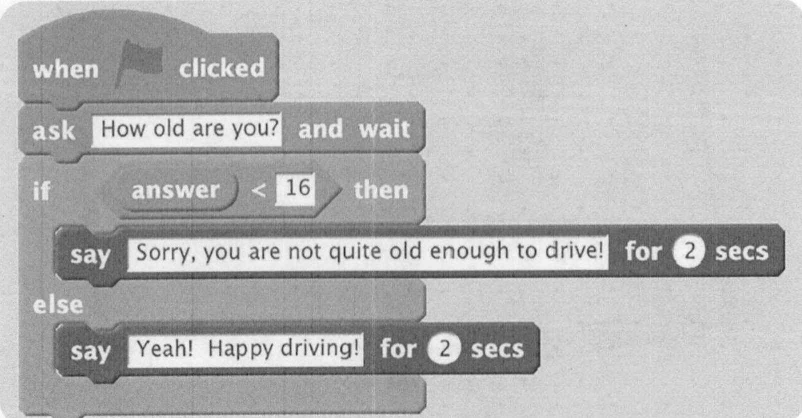

Figure 2.8

2.5.2 Limitations of Block Coding

- It is not suitable for every purpose.
- Debugging facilities are not available.
- On adding more functionalities, the number of blocks grows quickly, and the relationships between blocks become increasingly obscured.

Factz Funda

Google's Blockly' is a platform that produces working code in a variety of traditional programming languages, like JavaScript, PHP, etc. Thus, it makes it possible to experiment with blocks and immediately see the results in the desired programming language.

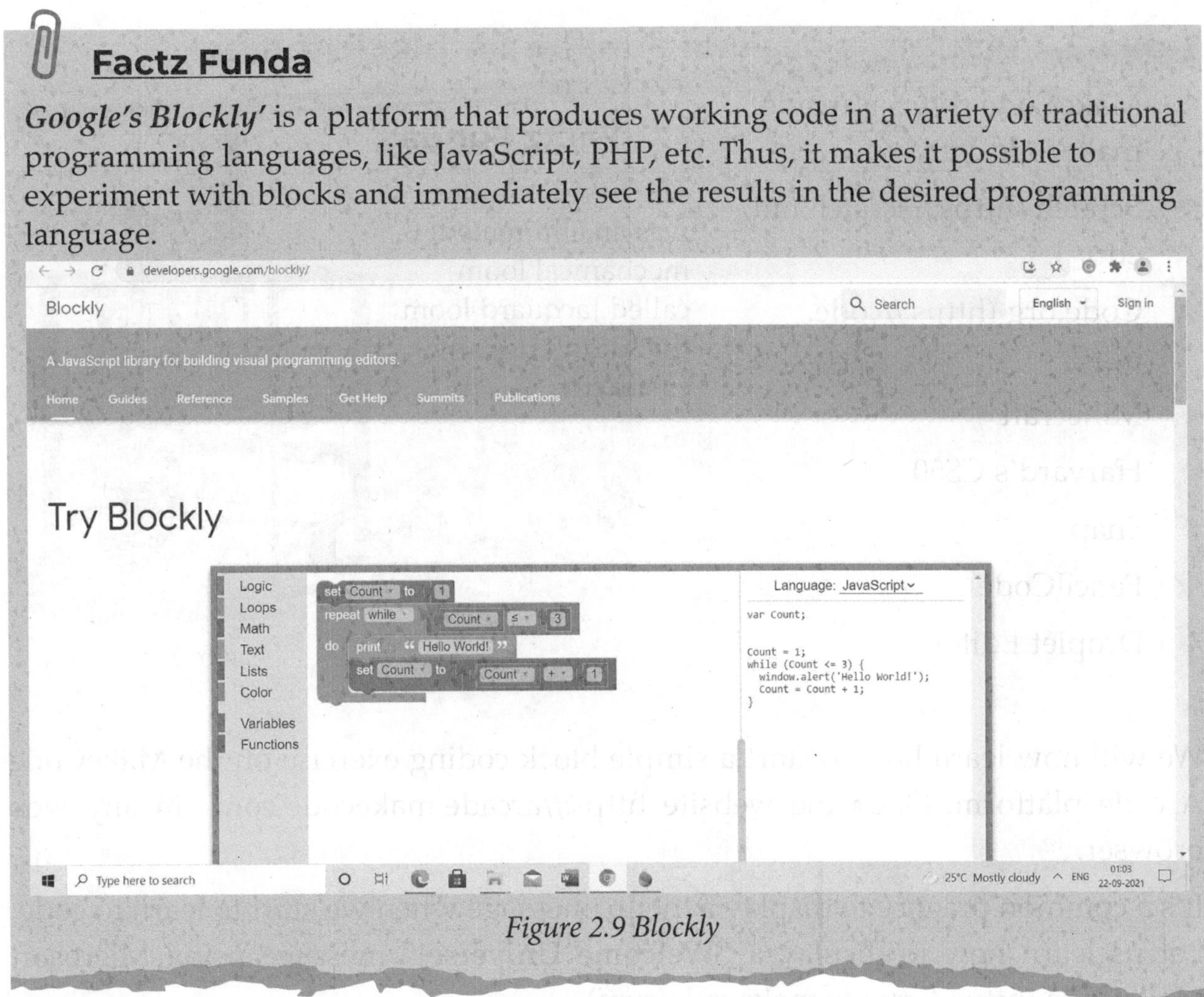

Figure 2.9 Blockly

2.6 GETTING STARTED WITH BLOCK CODING

MakeCode, developed by Microsoft, is a framework for creating interactive and engaging programming experiences for new learners of programming. The main objective of MakeCode is to bring programming to the forefront in such a way that becomes more attractive and friendly. To achieve this goal, MakeCode utilizes the blocks programming model to let learn coding concepts easily.

MakeCode Arcade is one of the platforms that are used to perform block-based programming. By using the 'arcade' platform, a solution to a problem can be implemented using various categories of blocks. Moreover, the results can be seen side by side on the same screen. The different categories of blocks will be discussed in the upcoming chapters. A list of online platforms available for block coding is provided in Table 2.2.

Table 2.2 Platforms available online for block coding

- MakeCode (https://arcade.makecode.com)
- Scratch (https://scratch.mit.edu/),
- Code.org (https://code.org/),
- Minecraft
- Harvard's CS50
- Snap
- PencilCode
- Droplet Editor

Factz Funda

The first computer was an automated, mechanical loom called Jacquard loom that didn't use any electricity.

Figure 2.10

We will now learn how to start a simple block coding exercise on the MakeCode Arcade platform. Open the website https://arcade.makecode.com in any web browser.

It's a common practice to display a 'hello' message when we start to learn to code. Let us learn how to display a **"Welcome Universe!"** message using Microsoft MakeCode (https://arcade.makecode.com).

The following steps will be used:

1. Open MakeCode arcade home screen.

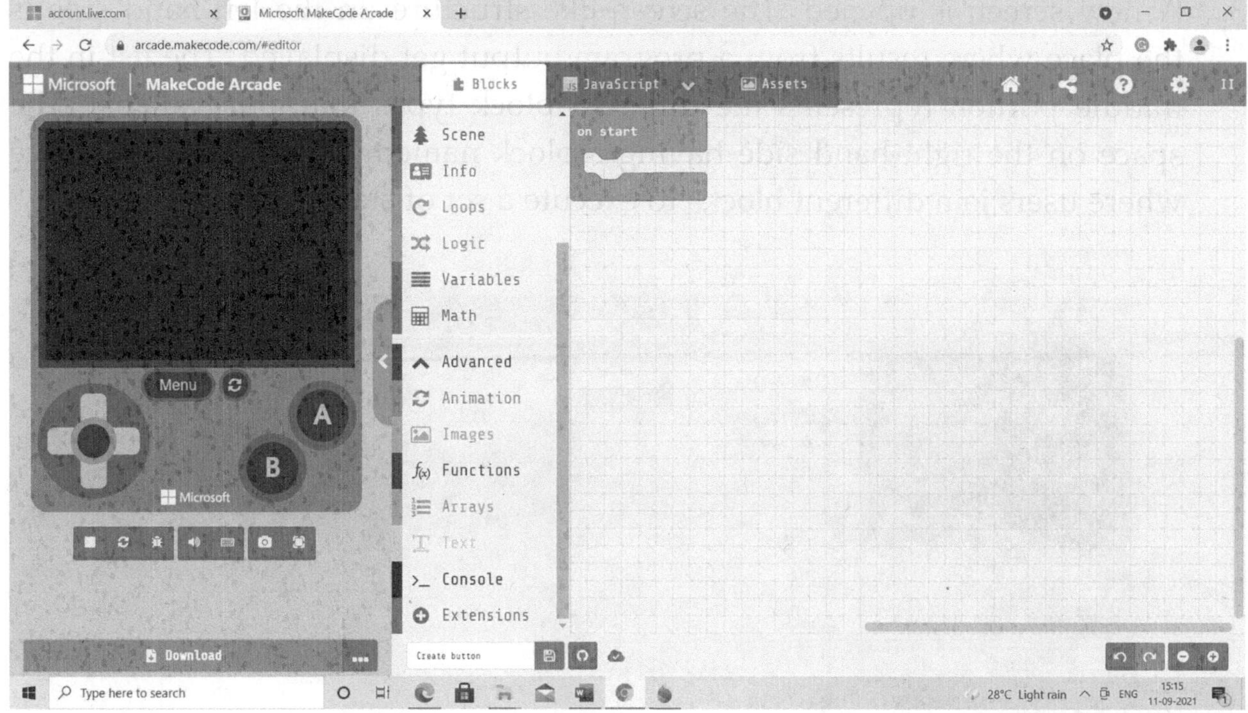

Figure 2.11

2. Click on new projects and name it "Greetings."

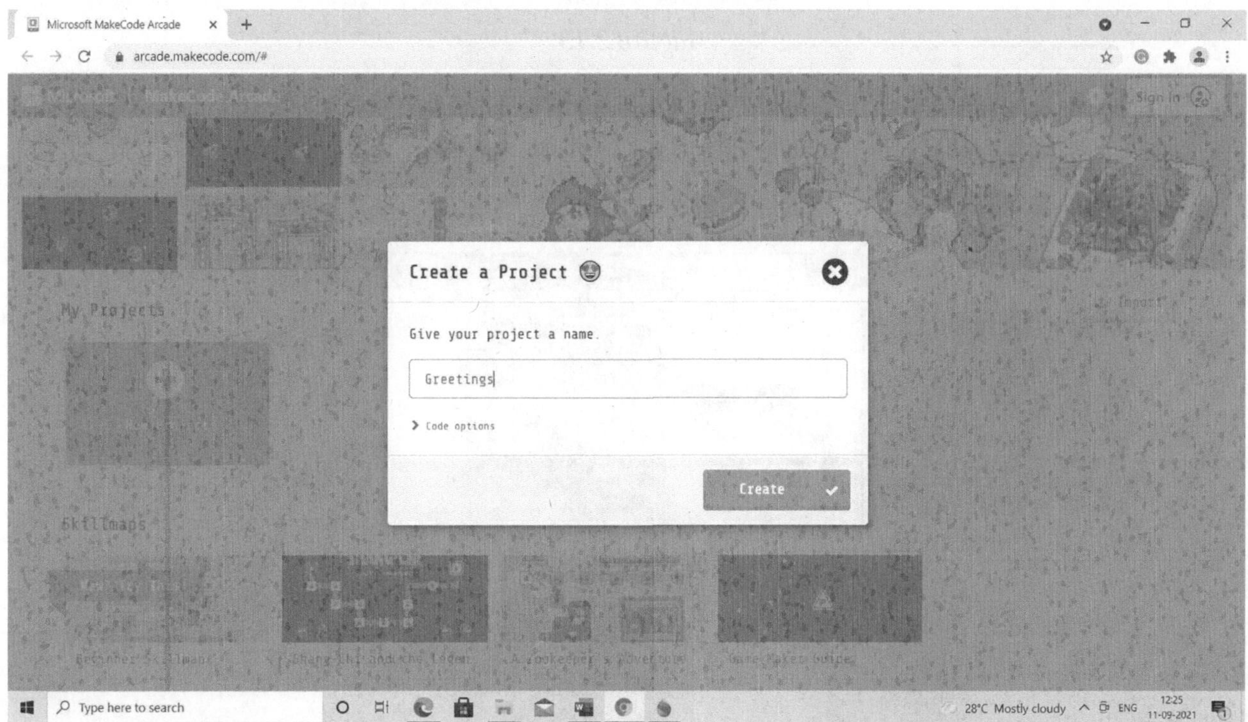

Figure 2.12

3. A new screen is opened. The screen-like structure on the left-hand side is the place where results from a program output get displayed. The list in the middle portion represents the different block types that are available. The space on the right-hand side having a block named "On start" is the place where users join different blocks to execute a set of steps/instructions.

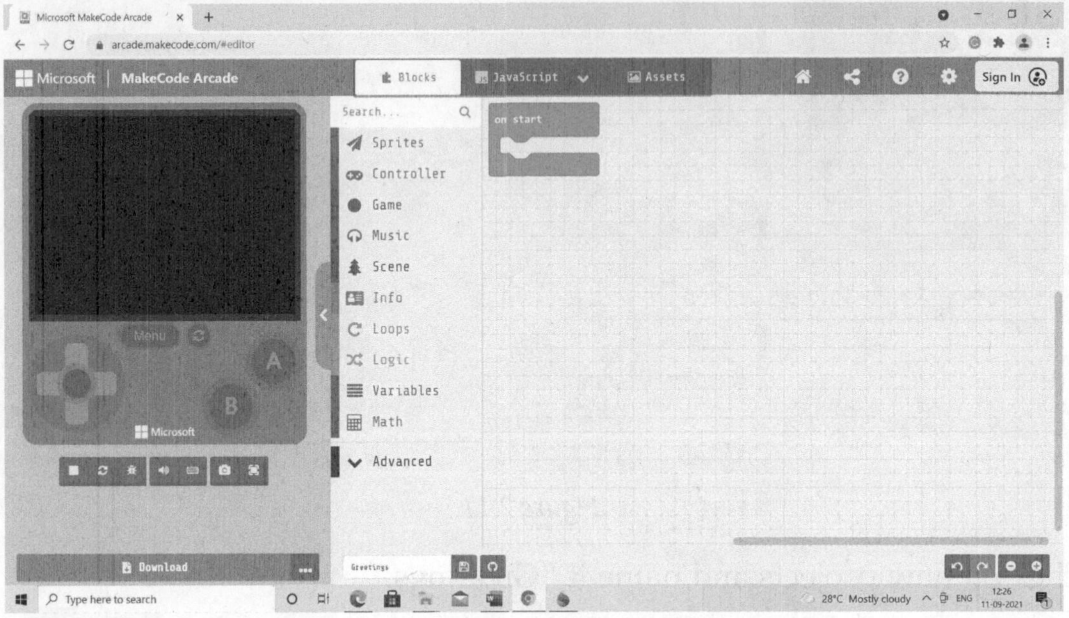

Figure 2.13

4. Go to the block type "Game" and select the block "Splash" as highlighted in the diagram.

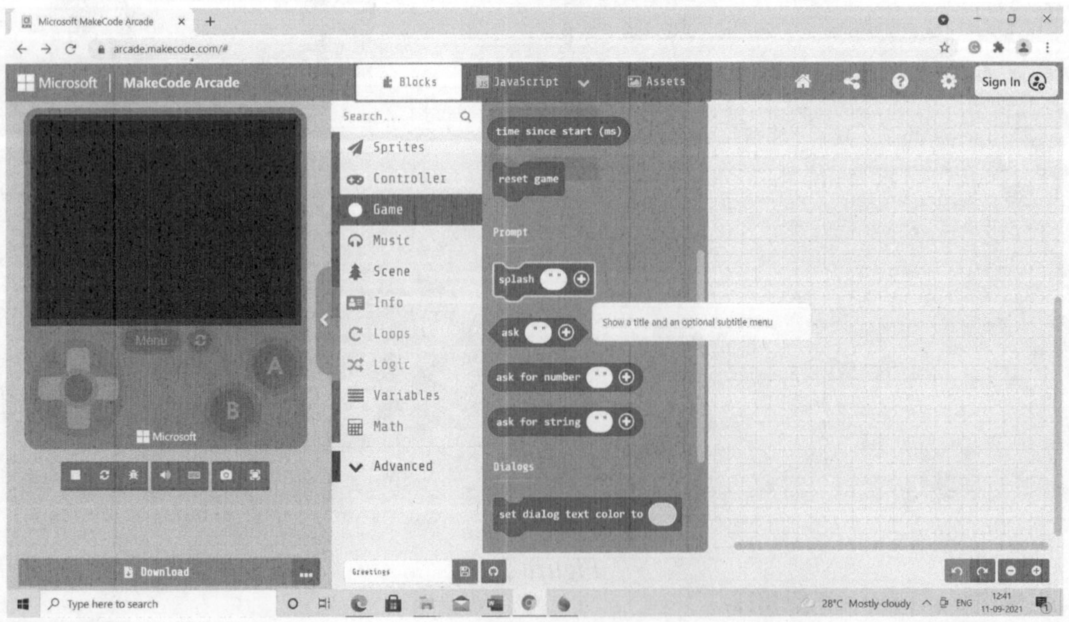

Figure 2.14

5. A separate block gets created in the space of the right-hand side as highlighted with yellow colour.

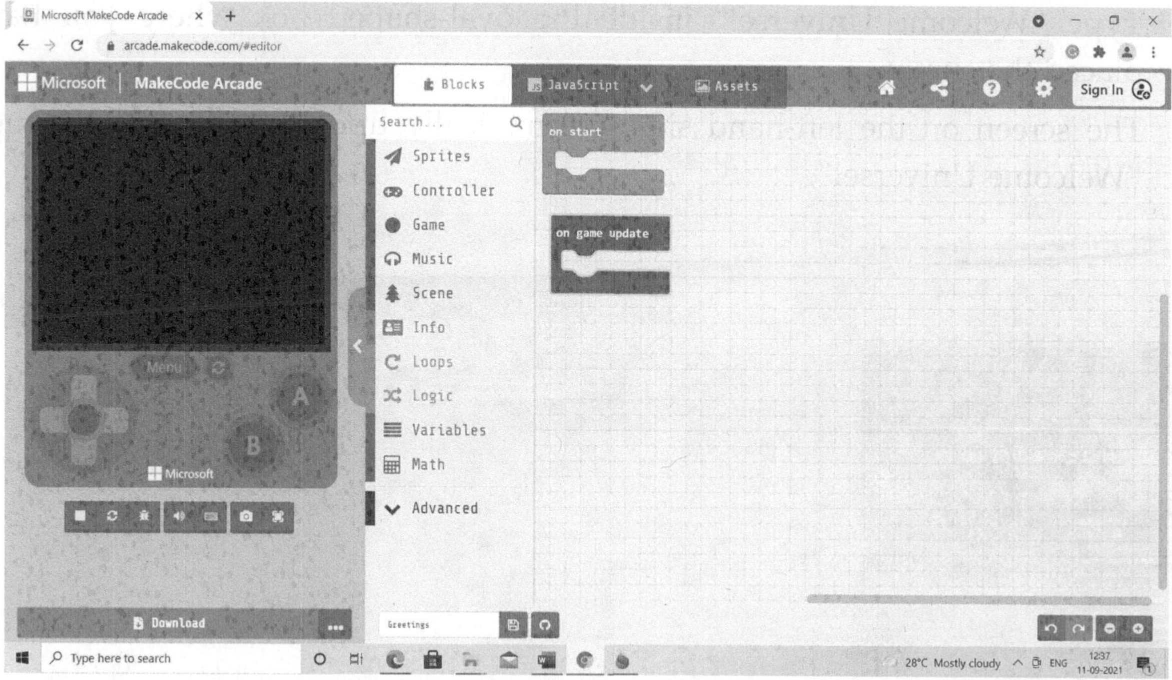

Figure 2.15

6. Drag and drop the new block inside the "On start" block. As soon as the "splash" block is placed inside the "On start" block, the display on the left-hand side screen changes.

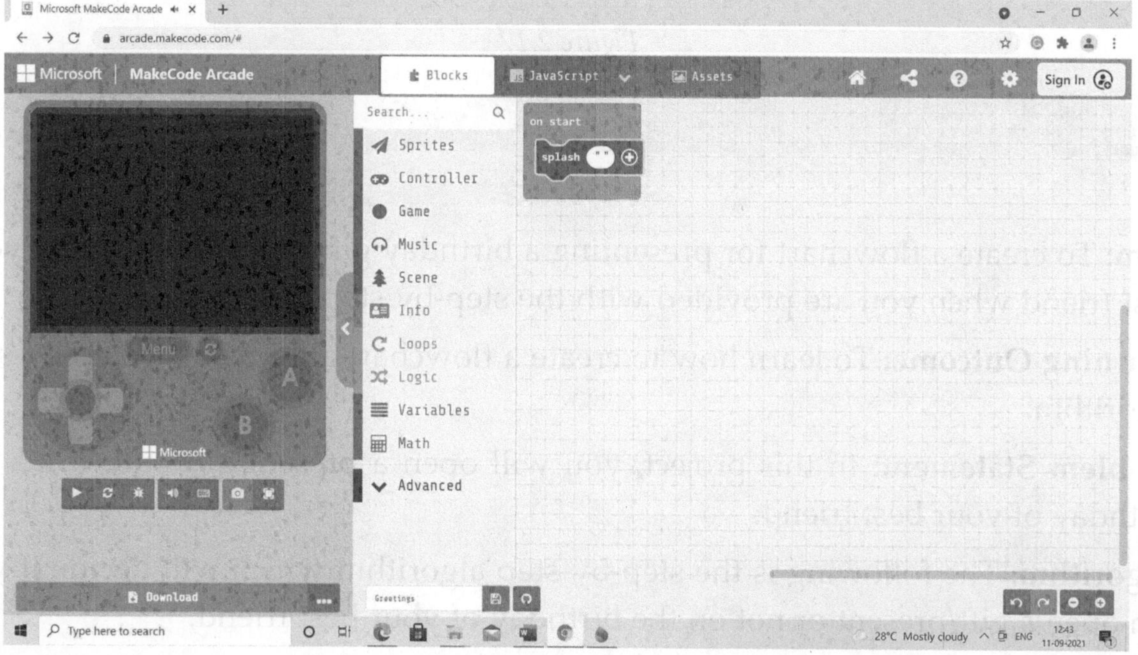

Figure 2.16

7. Left-click the mouse/pointer inside the oval-shaped area having the symbol of ". "
8. Type "Welcome Universe!" inside the oval-shaped box where you have placed the cursor.
9. The screen on the left-hand side automatically updated with the message "Welcome Universe!".

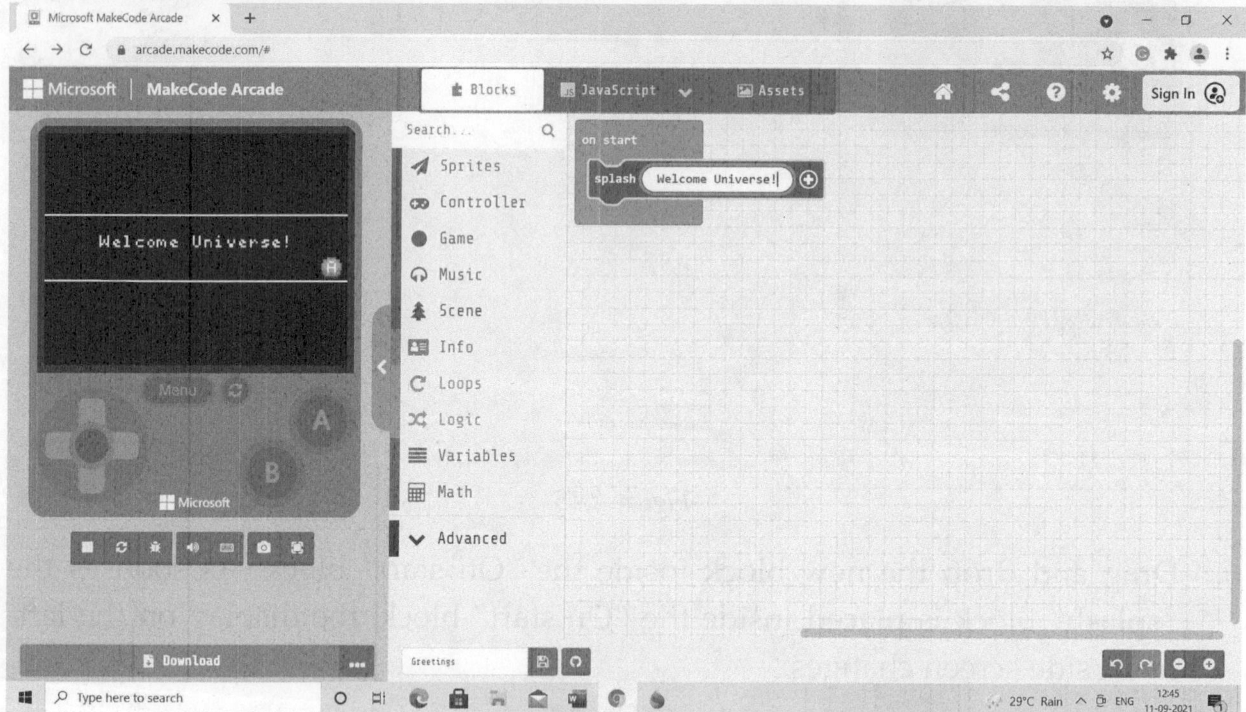

Figure 2.17

Project Time

Project 2.1

Aim: To create a flowchart for presenting a birthday gift on the birthday of your best friend when you are provided with the step-by-step algorithm.

Learning Outcome: To learn how to create a flowchart after using a step-by-step algorithm.

Problem Statement: In this project, you will open a present/gift only if it's the birthday of your best friend.

Algorithm: The following is the step-by-step algorithm which will decide if you can open a gift/present or not on the birthday of your best friend.

Step by step algorithm:

- Start
- Input the birthday of your best friend (Month and date).
- Input the present date.
- Whether Check to see today's date and month is equal to the birthday of your best friend.
- If yes, then you can present a birthday gift.
- If not, then check again every day till it's the birthday of your best friend.
- End

Using the above step-by-step algorithm, create a flowchart for the situation where you can present a birthday gift only if it's the birthday of your best friend.

Solution: A flowchart to present a birthday gift if it is the birthday of your best friend only; the following Flowchart may be drawn using the given step-by-step algorithm for the above situation:

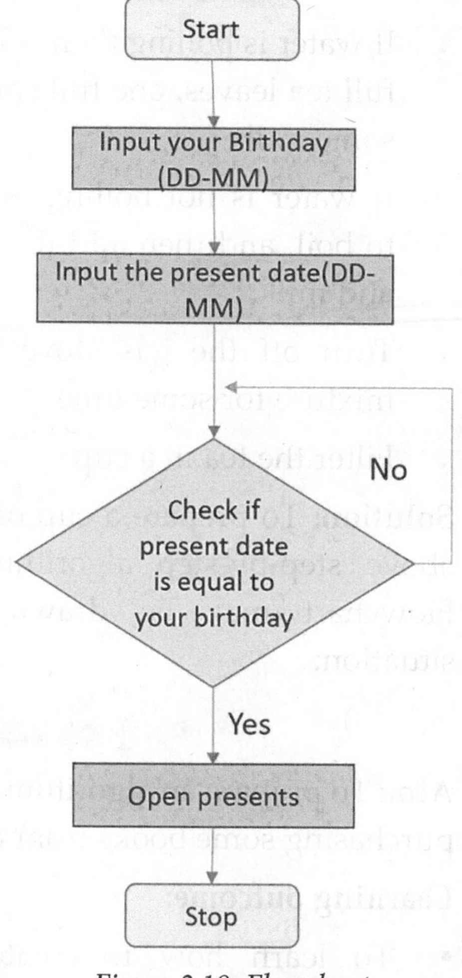

Figure 2.18: Flowchart

Project 2.2

Aim: To write a step-by-step algorithm and draw a flowchart for making a cup of tea.

Learning Outcome: To learn how to create a flowchart by using an algorithm.

Problem Statement: In this project you will learn how to make a cup of tea and how to draw a flowchart for the same by using the given step-by-step algorithm.

Algorithm: The following is the step-by-step algorithm for preparing a cup of tea.

Step-by-step algorithm:

- Take an appropriate quantity of water in the kettle/tea pan.
- Turn on the gas stove and put the cattle on the flame.

❖ Check to see if water is boiling or not.

❖ If water is boiling then, add half a teaspoon full tea leaves, one full spoon of sugar, and some milk.

❖ If water is not boiling, wait for the water to boil, and then add the tea leaves, sugar, and milk.

❖ Turn off the gas stove after boiling the mixture for some time.

❖ Filter the tea in a cup

Solution: To prepare a cup of tea by using the above step-by-step algorithm, the following Flowchart may be drawn for the above situation:

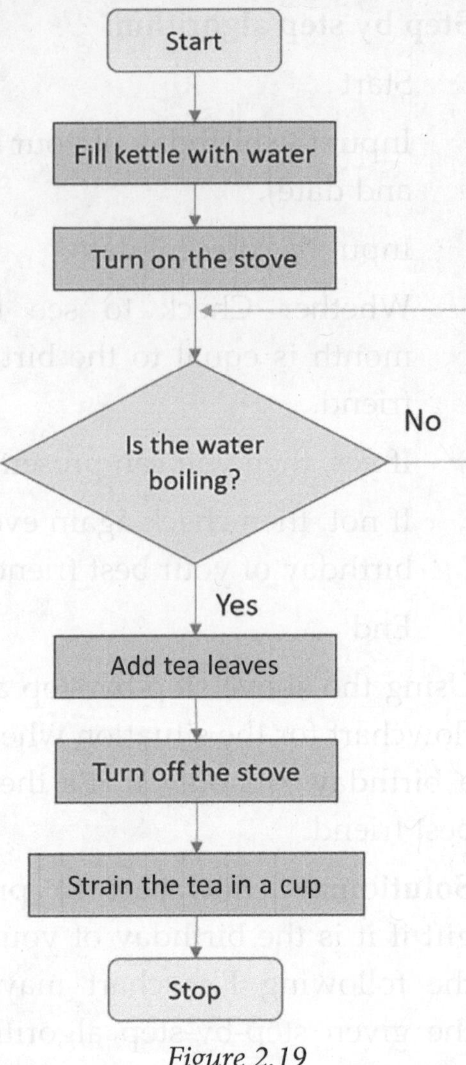

Figure 2.19

Project 2.3

Aim: To prepare an algorithm and flowchart for purchasing some books from an online store.

Learning outcome:

- To learn how to create a step-by-step algorithm for making an online purchase.
- To learn how to draw a flowchart using the algorithm you write.

Problem Statement: Suppose you need some books for your project and your parents have given you permission for online purchasing of books. You have to need to create a step-by-step algorithm and draw a flowchart for the algorithm.

Solution: The following is the step-by-step algorithm for purchasing books online.

Step-by-step algorithm:

❖ Enter

❖ Go to a website dealing in the online supply of books, like Amazon.

❖ Are you a registered user of this website?

❖ If you are not a registered user, then sign up and then sign in to the website.

- If you are a registered user, then sign in.
- Search for the required books.
- Are the books available?
- If the books are not available on the website, go back to the first step.
- If yes, Add the selected books to the cart.
- Review your order for its correctness.
- Select the payment method.
- Enter the information.
- If the entered information is correct, place an order.
- If not, then make changes and check again if the information entered is correct, and then place an order.
- End

The following Flowchart may be drawn based on the above step-by-step algorithm:

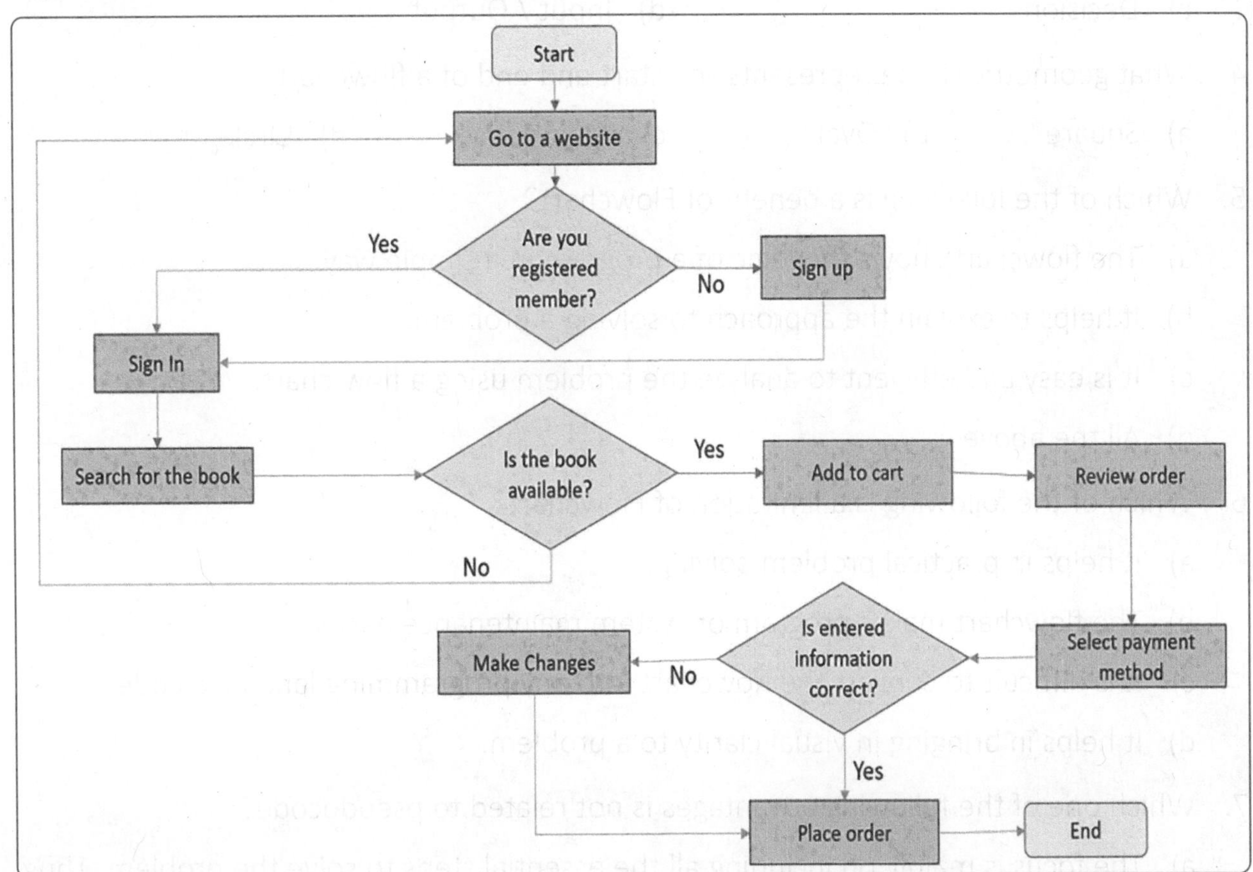

Figure 2.20: Flowchart

Tick (✓) the correct option.

1. What is a flowchart?
   a) A specific programming language
   b) A bullet point list of instructions
   c) A diagram representing a set of instructions
   d) A text-based way of designing an algorithm
2. Which of the following is not an advantage of a flowchart?
   a) Efficient coding b) Systematic testing
   c) Improper documentation d) Better communication
3. The arrows in a flowchart denote:
   a) Connectors b) Initialization
   c) Decision d) Input / Output
4. What geometric shape represents the start and end of a flowchart?
   a) Square b) Oval c) Diamond d) Circle
5. Which of the following is a benefit of Flowchart?
   a) The flowchart shows the logic of a program in a simple way.
   b) It helps to explain the approach to solving a problem.
   c) It is easy and efficient to analyze the problem using a flow chart.
   d) All the above
6. Which of the following is a limitation of Flowchart?
   a) It helps in practical problem-solving.
   b) The flowchart makes program or system maintenance easier.
   c) It is difficult to convert the flowchart into any programming language code.
   d) It helps in bringing in visual clarity to a problem.
7. Which one of the following advantages is not related to pseudocode?
   a) The focus is mainly on including all the essential steps to solve the problem. Thus, the solution tends to be comprehensive.

b) Since the user is not worried about coding syntax, he/she can concentrate on the actual problem.

c) It does not work as documentation of the code.

d) Reviewers can quickly review it and verify if the steps will generate the desired outcome.

8. Which of the following is not a platform for learning block coding?

   a) MakeCode b) Scratch c) decode.org d) PencilCode

9. Which of the following is not an advantage of block coding?

   a) It teaches students how to take clear instructions.

   b) It helps the students in organizing their thoughts in the form of writing sequences.

   c) It is easy to visualize the abstract ideas of programs in the form of blocks.

   d) It is easy on block coding to practice coding concepts and computational thinking.

10. In which web browser does the URL https://arcade.makecode.com open?

   a) Chrome b) Firefox c) Safari d) Any web browser

ANSWERS									
1. (c)	2. (c)	3. (a)	4. (b)	5. (d)	6. (c)	7. (c)	8. (c)	9. (a)	10. (d)

SUMMARY

- A program is a collection of instructions to perform a specific task when executed by a computer.
- A sequence of steps to solve any particular problem is called an algorithm.
- A flowchart is a diagrammatic representation of the step-by-step plan to be followed for solving a task/problem statement.
- Boxes in a flowchart show the process operations, the various steps, and actions.
- Arrows in a flowchart show the order of the steps and/or different options.
- The pseudocode in computer science is a plain language description of all the steps of an algorithm.
- Block coding is a type of visual programming that represents code as blocks on a graphical interface.
- Pseudocode has no syntax of any programming language.
- MakeCode, developed by Microsoft, is a framework for creating interactive and engaging programming experiences for new learners of programming.

- Block coding is not regarded as a substitute for real (text-based) code.
- The main benefit of block-based coding is that it clarifies to the students how to give clear instructions and organize their thoughts in the form of writing sequences.
- Block coding helps young students practice coding concepts and computational thinking.
- The block approach makes it easy to start programming.
- The URL https://arcade.makecode.com can be opened in any web browser.

PRACTICE TIME

(A) True/False Type Questions

1. Coding is behind almost every machine that is powered by electricity.
2. A program is a set of instructions to be performed for the execution of a specific task by a computer.
3. The program is usually written in any language.
4. A sequence of steps to solve any particular problem is called an algorithm.
5. The first programming language was Python.
6. Block coding is a type of visual programming that represents codes as blocks on a graphical interface.
7. A flowchart is a diagrammatic representation of the step-by-step plan to be followed for solving a task/problem statement.
8. Each shape in a flowchart act as a step in the solution/product/output, and the arrows represent the direction of flow among the steps.
9. A flowchart is a step-by-step list of directions that need to be followed to solve a problem.
10. Boxes in a flowchart show the process operations, the various steps, and actions.

ANSWERS					
1. T	2. T	3. F(specific programming language)		4. T	5. F (Fortran)
6. T	7. T	8. T	9. F (algorithm)	10. T	

(B) Fill in the blanks

1. ____________ is a list of step-by-step directions that need to be followed to solve a problem.
2. Herman Goldstine and ____________ developed the flowcharts first time.

3. Boxes in a ____________ show the process operations, the various steps, and actions.

4. ____________ is a type of visual programming that represents codes as blocks on a graphical interface.

5. The ____________ in computer science is a plain language description of all the steps of an algorithm.

6. ____________ in a flowchart, showing the order of the steps and/or different options.

7. Block coding is not a ____________ for real (text-based) code.

8. The main benefit of ____________ is that it clarifies to the students how to give clear instructions and organize the thoughts in the form of writing sequences.

9. Pseudocode has no ____________ of any programming language.

10. Block coding helps young students practice ____________ concepts and computational thinking.

ANSWERS			
1. An algorithm	2. John von Neumann	3. Flowchart	4. Block coding
5. Pseudocode	6. Arrows	7. Substitute	8. block coding
9. Syntax	10. Coding		

(C) Very Short Answer Type Questions

1. What do you mean by a flowchart?
2. What is a pseudocode?
3. Which geometric shape is used to exhibit processing in a flowchart?
4. Which is sometimes called the "language of the future" as it has become the inevitable truth of the future?
5. Who developed flowcharts first time in the world?

(D) Short Answer Type Questions

1. What are the benefits of using flowcharts?
2. Write three benefits of using flowcharts.
3. Write two limitations of block coding.
4. Write the purpose of each type of box used in a flowchart.
5. State a problem and write a flowchart for it.

(E) Higher Order Thinking Skills (HOTS)

1. Why are pseudocodes used?
2. How is a flowchart useful for a new programmer?

(F) Projects

1. Create a flowchart based on your normal school day. Here are some guidelines:

   Getting ready for school

   - Look at your timetable and pack your school bag.
   - If Mass PT is there, then packing your Mass PT uniform and shoes.

   At school

   - Attend the morning assembly.
   - Attend a session with subjects Math, English, and science.
   - A decision on what to play during recess.

   After reaching home

   - Have snacks.
   - Depending on the day, choose the class you have to attend:
     Monday-Karate, Tuesday-Math Class, Wednesday and Thursday Free day, Friday-Karate

2. Write an algorithm and draw its Flowchart to find the average of three numbers.

3 Variables Using Block Coding

Structure

In this chapter, you will learn:

- What are variables?
- How to name variables?
- Commonly used data types
- Performing operations on variables
- Assignment

INTRODUCTION

Variables in a computer program are similar to 'Buckets' or 'Envelopes,' where information can be maintained and referenced. We write a name on the outside of the envelope/bucket for its identification. When we are referring to the bucket/envelope, we use the name of the bucket/envelope, not the data stored in the bucket. Thus, variables are 'Symbolic Names,' and the variable "stands in" for any possible values.

In this chapter, we shall study variables and data types in detail and perform some operations on variables using block coding.

Figure 3.1

Learning Objectives:

At the end of this chapter, you will be able to know:

- What are variables, and how they are used in programming.
- Ways of naming variables.
- Different data types in programming and their usage.
- Various operations that we can perform of different data types in programming.

3.1 VARIABLES

A variable is defined as a named location that is used to store data in the memory of the computer. We assume the variable as a container (like envelope or bucket) holding data that can be changed later throughout programming. For example,

$$x = 42, y = 24$$

The above declarations make sure that the program reserves memory for two variables with the names x and y. The variable names stand for the memory location. Thus, in programming, a variable is a packet that can store data. These packets can be named and referenced and can be used to perform various operations. To perform a mathematical operation, you can declare two or more variables and perform the operation on them.

Scope of a variable normally refers to the part of the code where the variable can be used. The scope or accessibility of the variables defined in a program depends on where you have declared it in each program. Any defined variable cannot be accessed beyond its scope.

Variables

What are they?

- A storage location for data in a computer program
- The storage location can be used to store a value and used to retrieve the value
- E.g., "player 1 name" is the name of the variable which contains the name typed in by the user

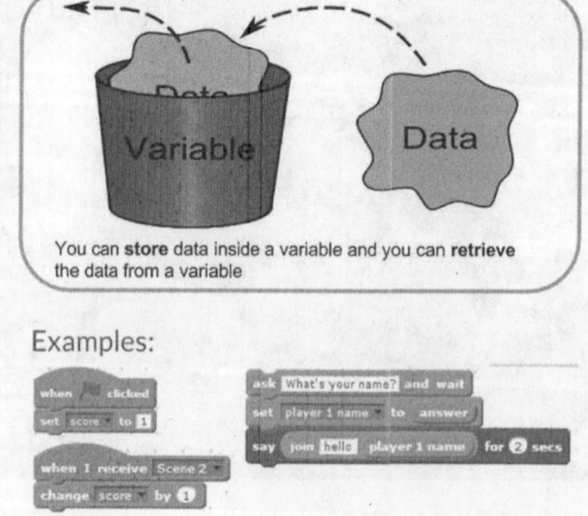

Figure 3.2

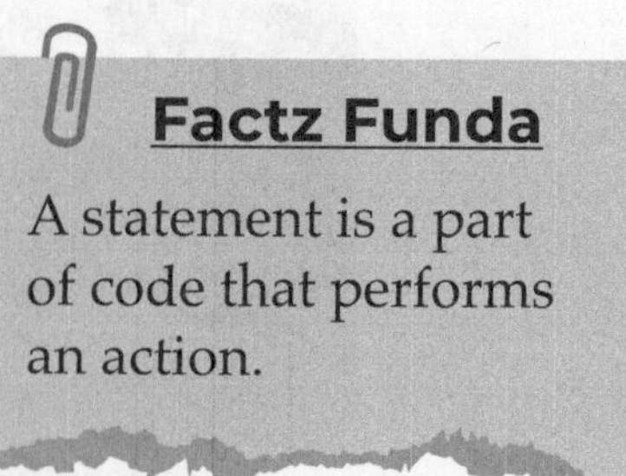

3.3 NAMING VARIABLES

Now, we have understood that variables are basically like nouns in a programming language. Each and every variable in a program is unique. To identify these variables uniquely, the user needs to name them in a unique manner. The given name acts as an identifier for that variable. In programming, a user is not allowed to use the same name of a variable more than once. Naming variables make it easier to call them while performing operations. The name of a variable also suggests what information the variable contains.

Figure 3.3

Consider this example for a better understanding of variables:

If variable named as "a" is equal to 6 and variable named as "b" is equal to 7, performing add operation on "a" and "b" is going to result in output as "13".

3.3.1 Rules and Naming convention for variables

- Create a name that makes sense. For example, vowel makes more sense than v.
- Use camelCase notation to declare a variable. It starts with a lowercase letter. For example: myName
- Using capital letters is possible to declare a constant. For example: PI
- Never use special symbols in naming variables, like * , !, @, #, $, %, etc.

3.4 DATA TYPES IN VARIABLES

Variables are the values that are acted upon. Every value needs to be assigned to a specific data type to make the variable more readable by a computer. Data type identifies the type of data that the declared variable can hold. Thus, it indirectly helps the computer to understand what operations need to be performed on those variables. The declaration of a variable in a program contains two components – the name of the variable and its type.

Figure 3.4

Let us now understand what the common data types that we can use in programming. These are given in Table 3.1.

Table 3.1 Common types in variables

- Integer
- Floating-point number
- Character
- String
- Boolean

(i) Integer Data Type

Integer data type variables store integer values only. They store whole numbers which have zero, positive and negative values but not decimal values. Multiple programming languages support different syntax to declare an Integer variable. If a user tries to create an integer variable and assign it a non-integer value, the program returns an error.

Examples of declaring an integer variable:

```
int a = 5;
int b = 3;
```

Variables of the integer data type are only capable of holding single values. These variables are not capable of holding a long list of values.

Factz Funda

A variable whose value cannot be changed even later on is called a 'Constant.'

(ii) Floating Point Number Data Type

Floating-point numbers are used to store decimal values. They hold real numbers with decimal values. Depending on the programming language, the syntax to declare floating-point variable changes.

Examples of declaring a floating -point number variable:

```
float a = 3.5;
float b = 8.3;
```

There is another type of floating-point number known as a "double" data type, which is used to store even bigger values.

Examples of declaring a double value:

```
float a = 5.888888888 * 6.333333333;
float b = 9.444444444 * 7.666666666;
```

(iii) Character Data Type

Character type variables are used to store character values. Syntax of declaring a character variable is specific to the programming language that you are using. If a user tries to create a character variable and assign it with a non-character value, the program will throw an error. The character data type is the smallest data type in programming.

Examples of declaring a character variable:

```
char a = 'P';
char b = 'S';
```

Any character value can be declared as a char variable.

(iv) String Data Type

To extend the character data type, a user may have a requirement to store and perform an operation on a sequence of characters. In such cases, the String data type is present to fit the gap. The String data type stores value in a sequence of characters, i.e., in String format. Any string value can be declared as a string variable.

Examples of declaring a string variable:

```
str a = "My name is SP Verma";
str b = "Beautiful India";
```

(v) Boolean Data Type

There is a subtype of Integer Data Type called "Boolean Data Type," which stores values in Boolean type only, i.e., "true" or "false." Users can choose between the data types for variables as per program needs and assign variables an appropriate data type.

Examples of declaring a boolean variable:

```
bool a = true;
bool b = false;
```

Boolean is a subtype of integer data type. It stores true and false where true means non-zero and false means zero. Any Boolean variable holding Boolean value can be declared as Boolean.

It is interesting to note that in some programming languages like Python, there is no command to declare variables. A variable is created the moment when the user first assign a value to it.

Examples of declaring variables in Python:

```
a = 8;
b = "Hi";
c = 5.9
```

When we want to specify the data type of variable, then this can be done using casting.

Example:

x = str("hello"),

y = int(7),

z = float(7.0)

x will be saved as 'hello'

y will be saved as 7

z will be saved as 7.0

Factz Funda

The numerical values which fall under integers or whole numbers are called discrete data types.

Now, we will learn how to apply different data types in pseudocode. We will first declare different types of variables, followed by assigning them to appropriate values. Finally, we will use the variables by outputting their values.

```
Function Main
Declare
.......................................
    Declare Integer i
    Declare Float f
    Declare Char c
    Declare String s
    Declare Boolean b
Assign
.......................................
    Assign i = 3456
```

```
    Assign f = 2.57
    Assign c = 'V'
    Assign s = "Parents love their children"
    Assign b = true
Use
....................................................................................
    Output "Integer i = " & i
    Output "Float f = " & f
    Output "Char c = " & c
    Output "String s = " & s
    Output "Boolean b = " & b
End
```

The output from the above pseudocode will be like as follows:

```
    Integer i = 3456
    Float f = 2.57
    Char c = 'V'
    String s = "Parents love their children"
    Boolean b = true
```

It should be noted that the syntax is different for different data types in other programming languages.

In Python, string variables may be declared either by single quotes or double quotes, or triple quotes. Below are some rules for naming a variable in Python:

- A variable name cannot start with a number; it must start with an alphabet or the underscore (_) sign.
- The variable name is case-sensitive. Thus, 'Sum' and 'sum' are different variables.
- A variable can only contain alphanumeric characters and underscore

3.5 PERFORMING OPERATIONS ON VARIABLES

Operators are special symbols that represent computation. They are applied to operand(s), which can be values or variables. Same operators can behave differently on different data types. Operators, when applied to operands, form an expression.

Figure 3.5

After declaring the data types in programming, now we will learn what operations we can perform on the data types and how do we perform these operations:

3.5.1 Arithmetic Operations

An arithmetic operation combines two or more numeric expressions using the Arithmetic Operators to form a resulting numeric expression. The basic operators for performing arithmetic are the same in many computer languages:

- Addition
- Subtraction
- Multiplication
- Division
- Modulus (Remainder)

(a) **Addition:** The addition arithmetic operation is used to add the values stored in one variable from another variable. Like the way we add values in mathematics, we can store values in different variables and perform addition operations. Additions of these variables is displayed as an output of the program.

Activity 3.1

- Participate in the individual activity on "**Addition operation using block coding.**"
- An addition arithmetic operation is used to add the values stored in two variables. Similar to adding values in mathematics, we store values in different variables and perform an additional operation. The addition of the variables is displayed as an output of the program.
- For example, performing addition operation on a variable "a" holding value "8" and a variable "b" holding value "9" will result in an output "17". To understand this arithmetic operation better, let us understand how to implement it practically in programming. For this, we are going to take an example of the platform https://arcade.makecode.com/ . Let us refer to the steps below to understand more in detail.

Step1: Open the MakeCode arcade home screen.

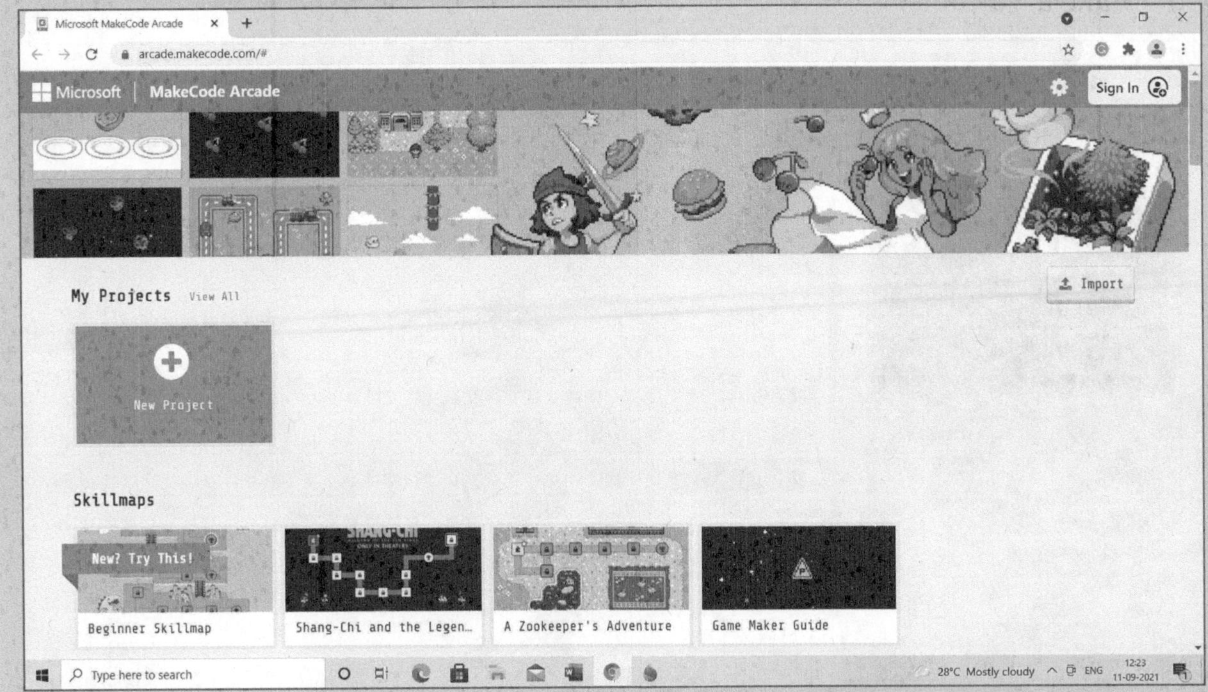

Figure 3.6

Step 2: Click on "New Project," give a name to the project and click on the"'create" button.

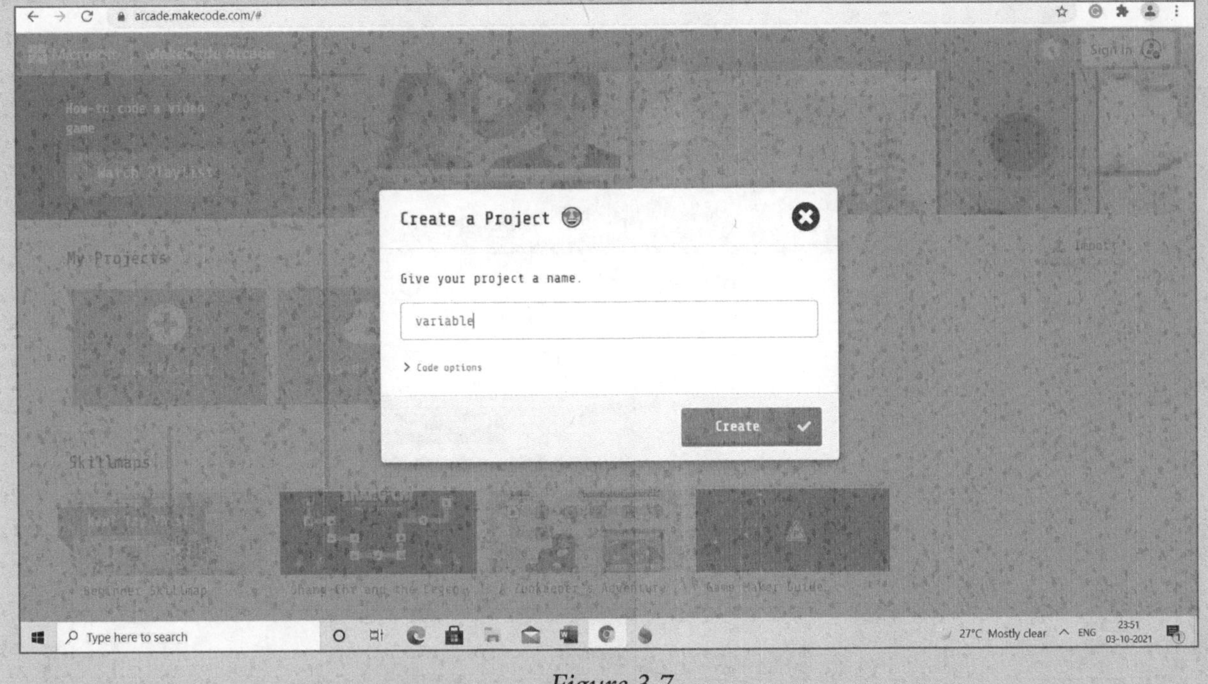

Figure 3.7

Step 3: From the list in the centre of the page, click on "Variables" and then click on "Make a Variable."

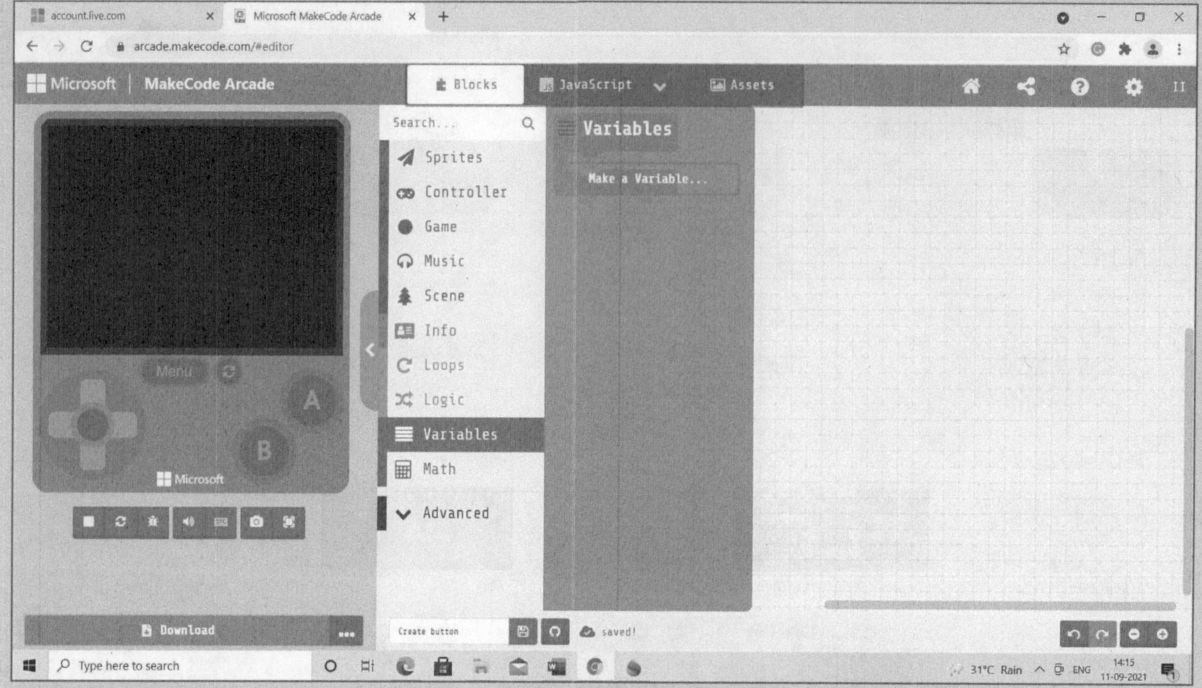

Figure 3.8

Step 4: Name the new variable as "a" and click on the "OK" button.

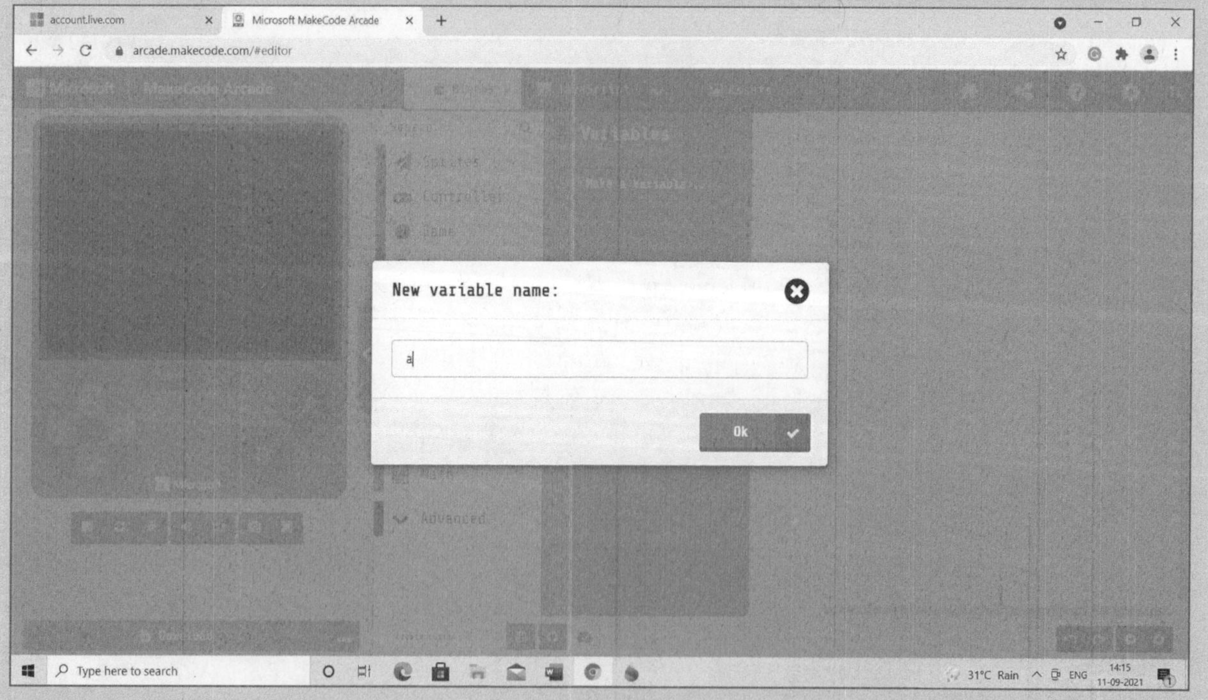

Figure 3.9

Step 5: Click on the value of "a" and change to the desired value. In this case, we are taking it as "20". Drag and drop "a" to the green block.

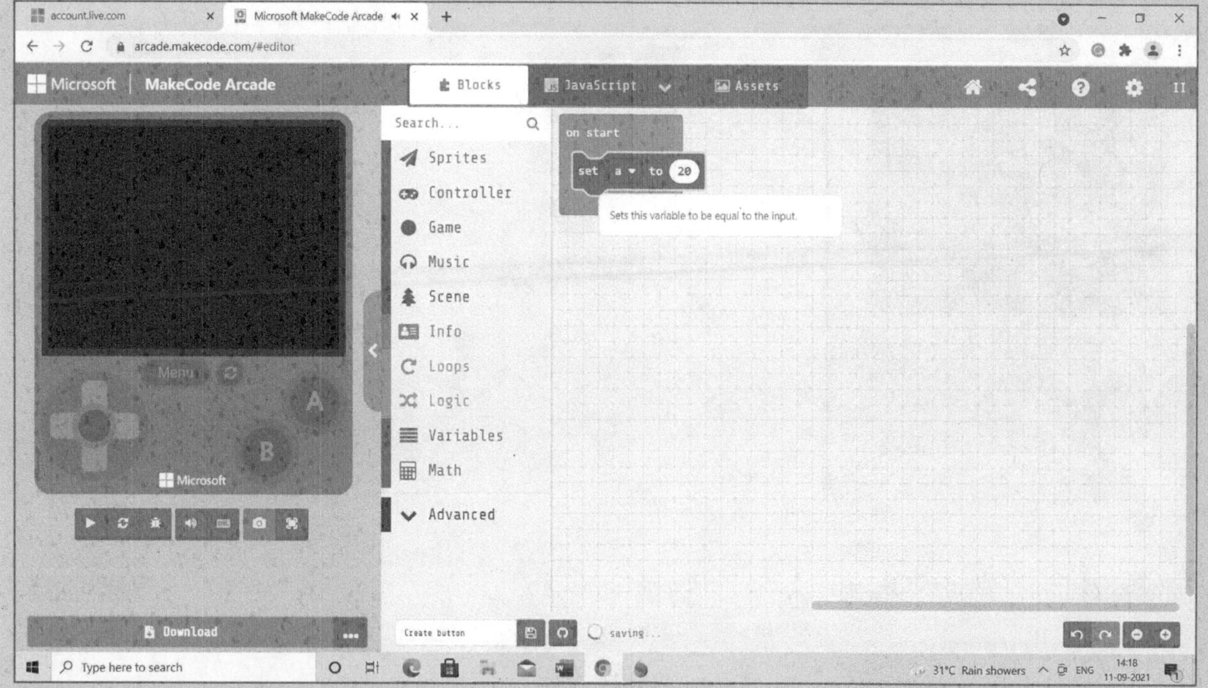

Figure 3.10

Step 6: Similarly, make another variable "b".

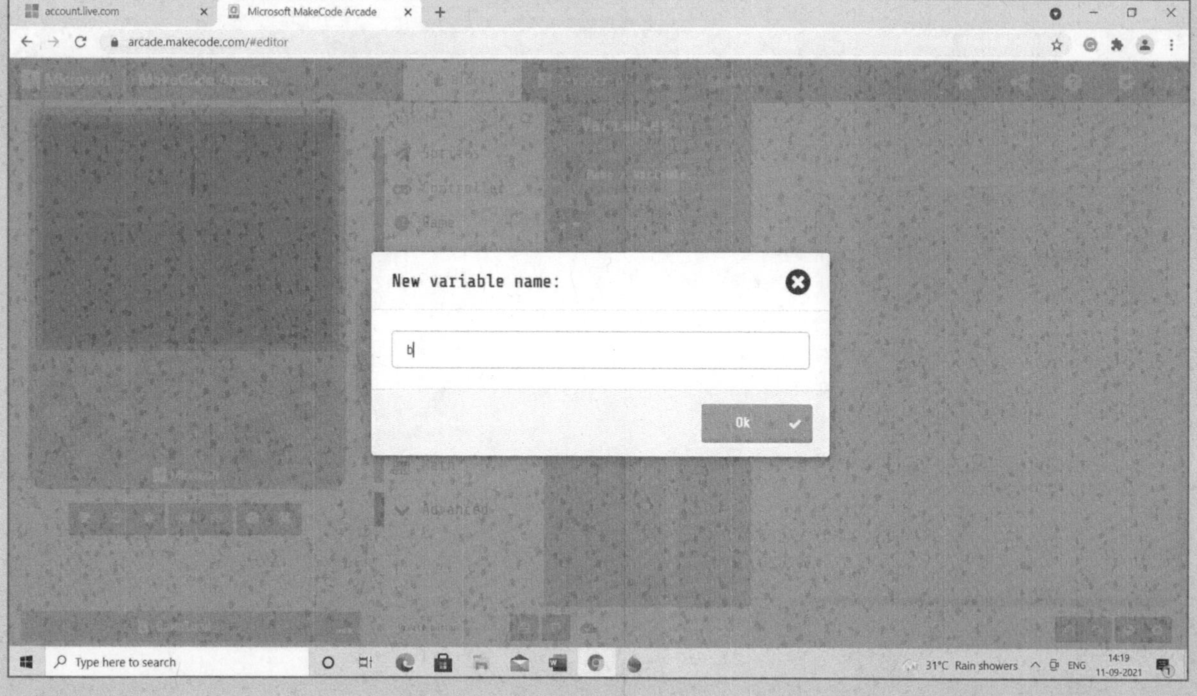

Figure 3.11

Step 7: Assign it a value "15",

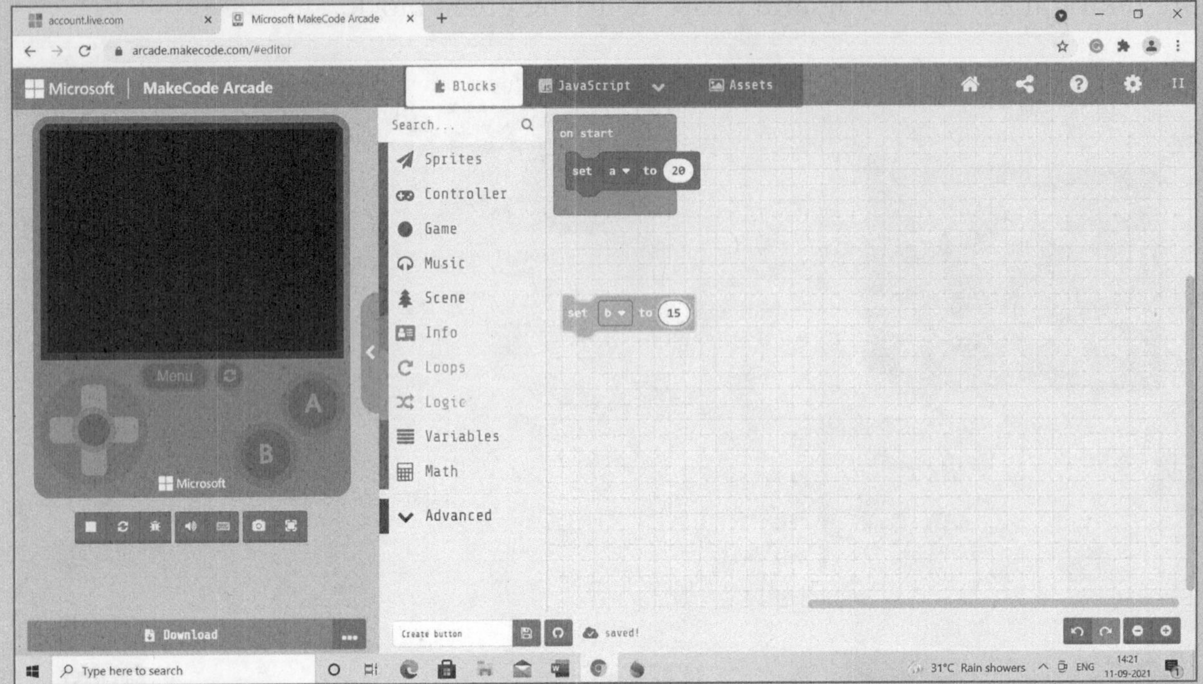

Figure 3.12

Step 8: Drag and drop variable b on the green block.

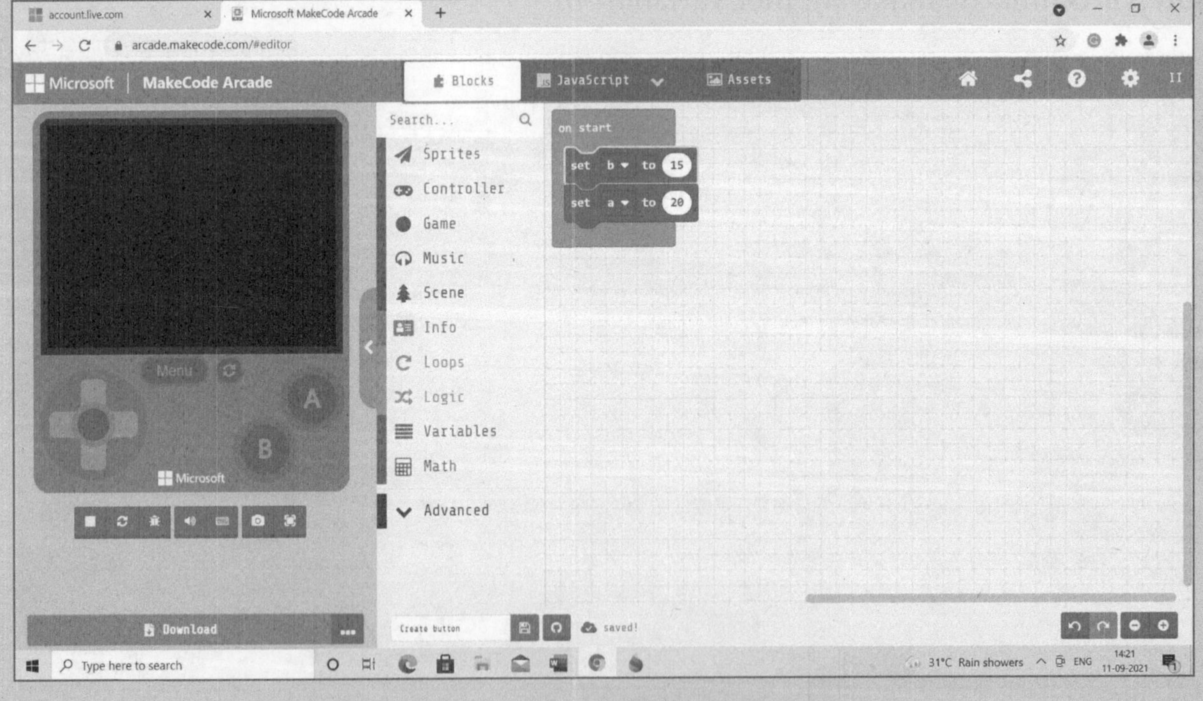

Figure 3.13

Step 8: Now, click on the "Math" link from the centre of the page and click on the addition operation.

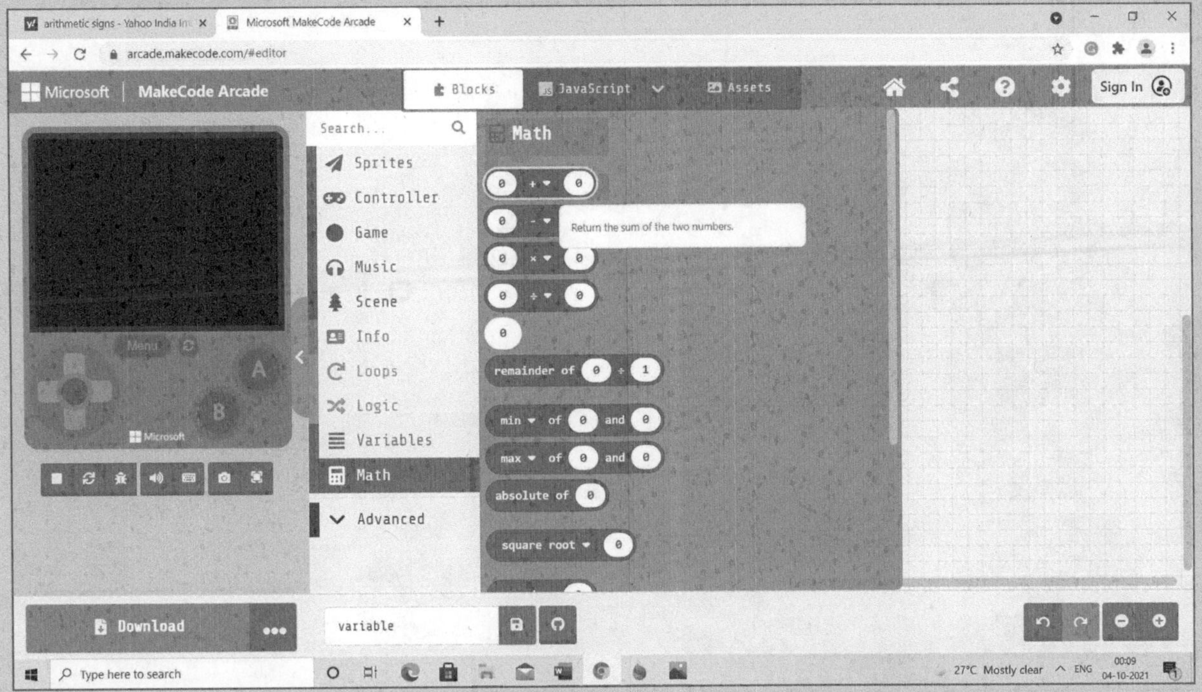

Figure 3.14

Step 9: Now, click on the "Variables" link from the centre of the page and drag and drop variables "a" and "b" in the addition box as seen in the screenshot.

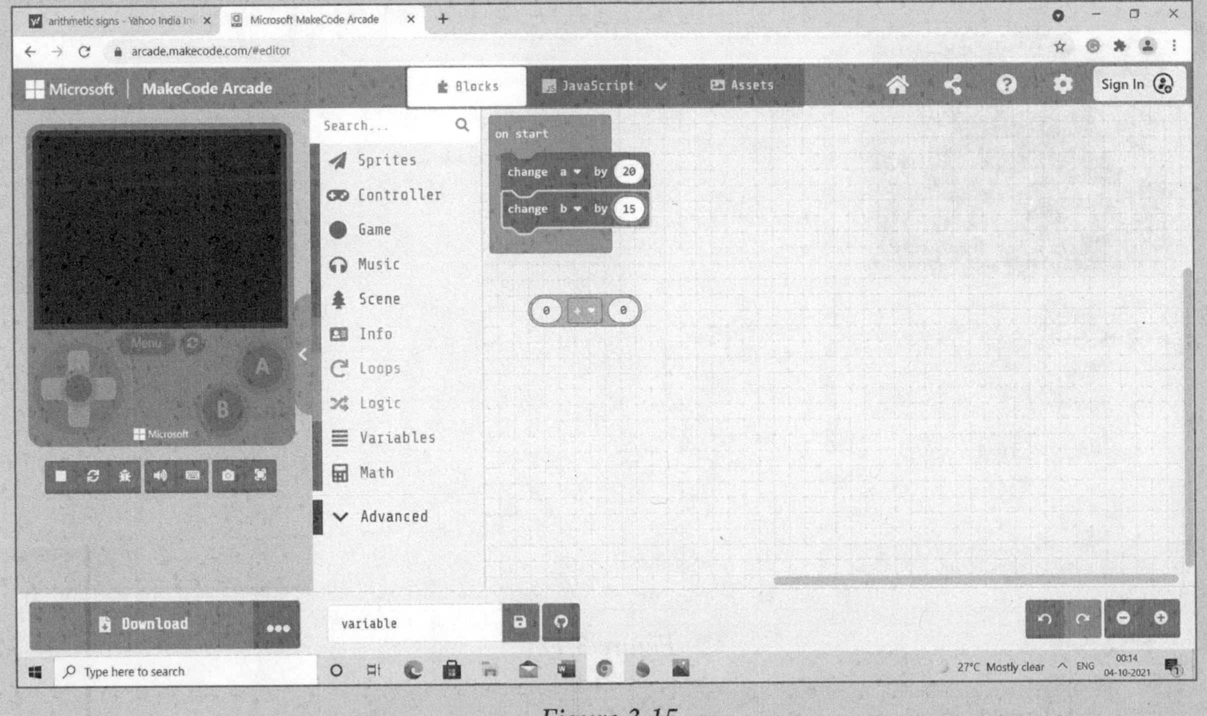

Figure 3.15

Step 10: Like the way we had created variables a and b, now create variable c. Drag and drop block of variable c to in the play area.

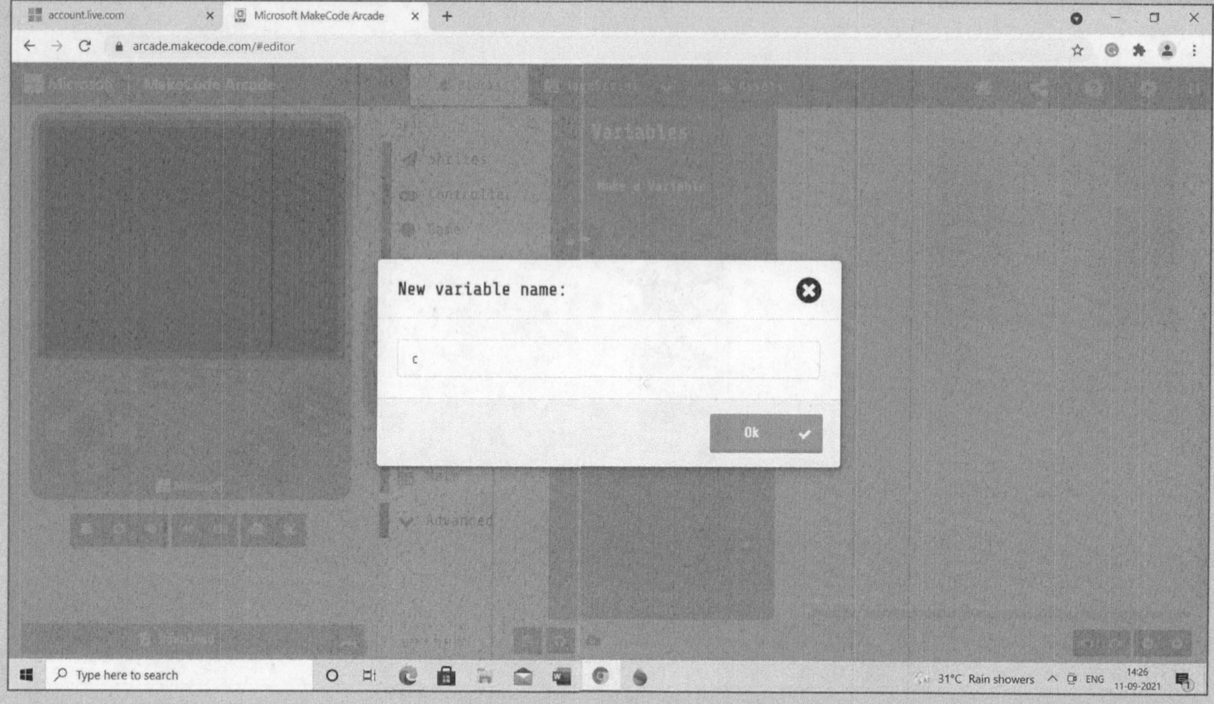

Figure 3.16

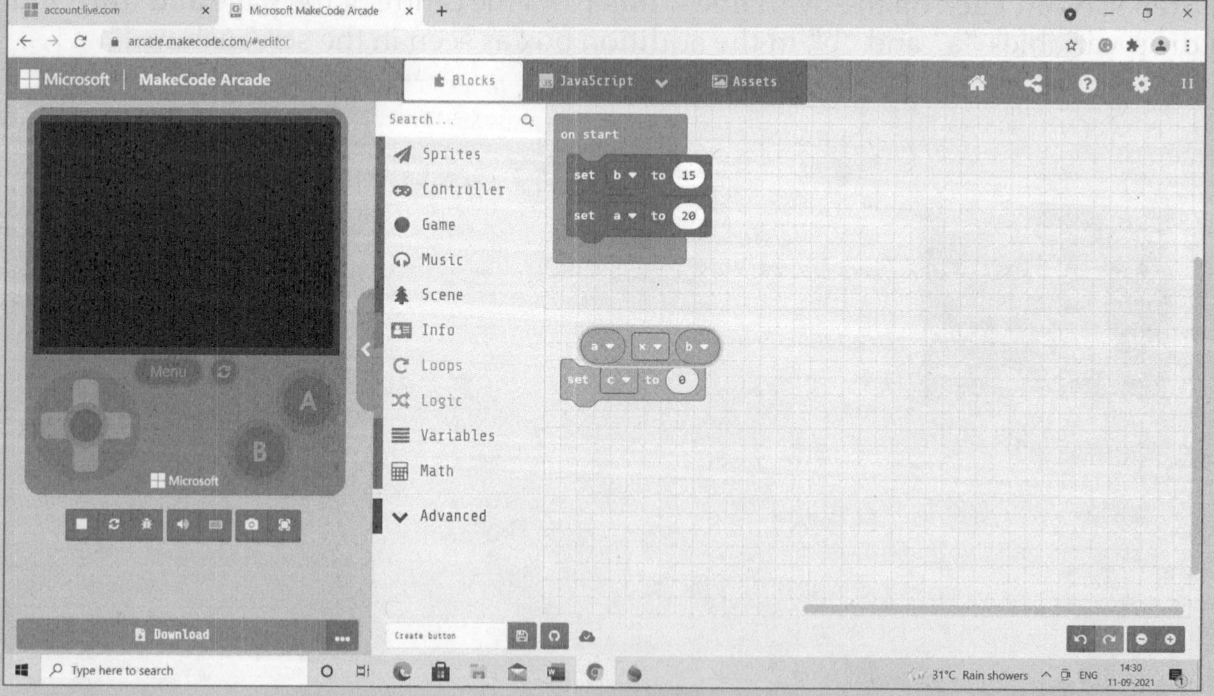

Figure 3.17

Step 11: Now, drag and drop the addition block in the set "c" to block as seen in the screenshot.

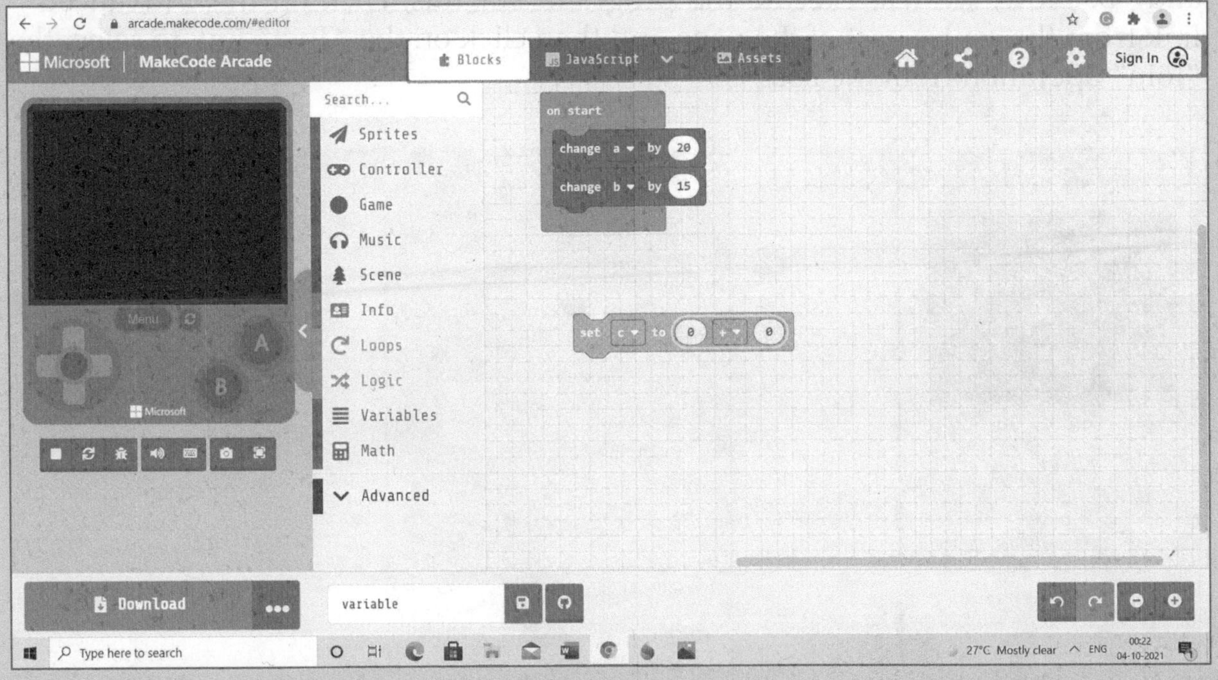

Figure 3.18

Step 12: Now, drag and drop the block of "set "c" to" to "a" + "b" in the green block.

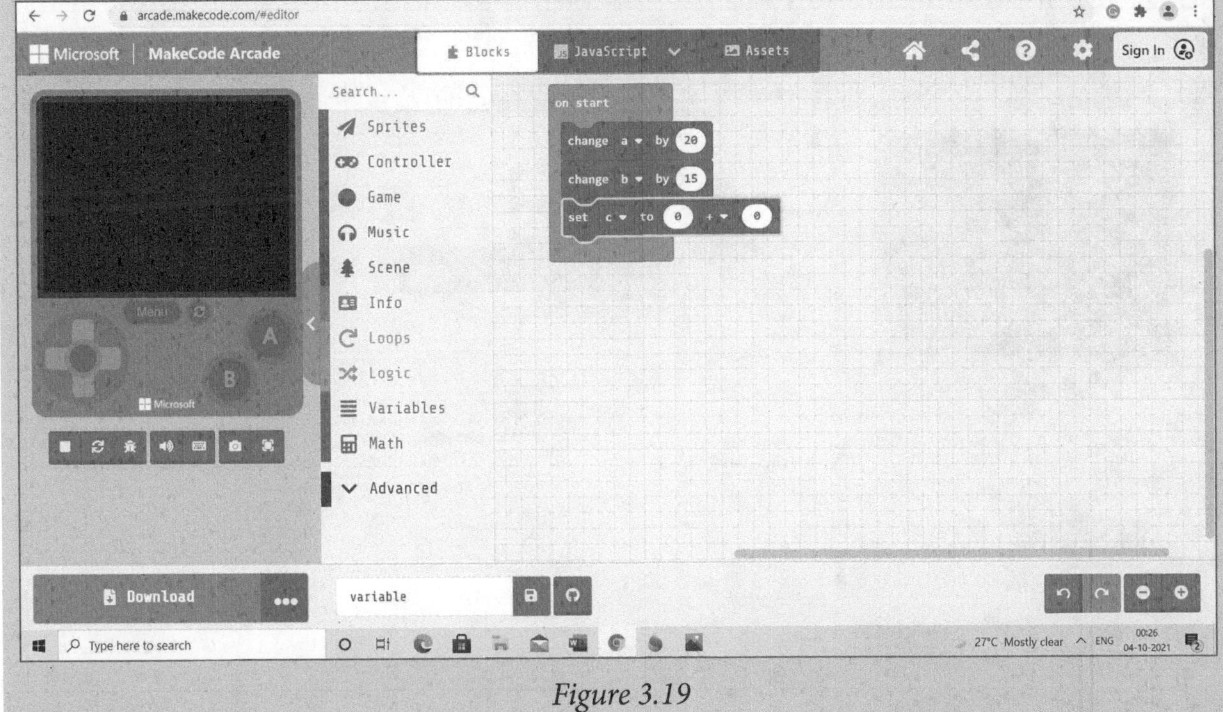

Figure 3.19

Step 13: We have created the variables and assigned them the values, and then created a third variable, "c," which will have the output of the addition of "a" and "b."Now, we will execute the program. For this, click on the "Advanced " link from the centre part of the page and then click on the "Text" link to select the "Join" operation from the list.

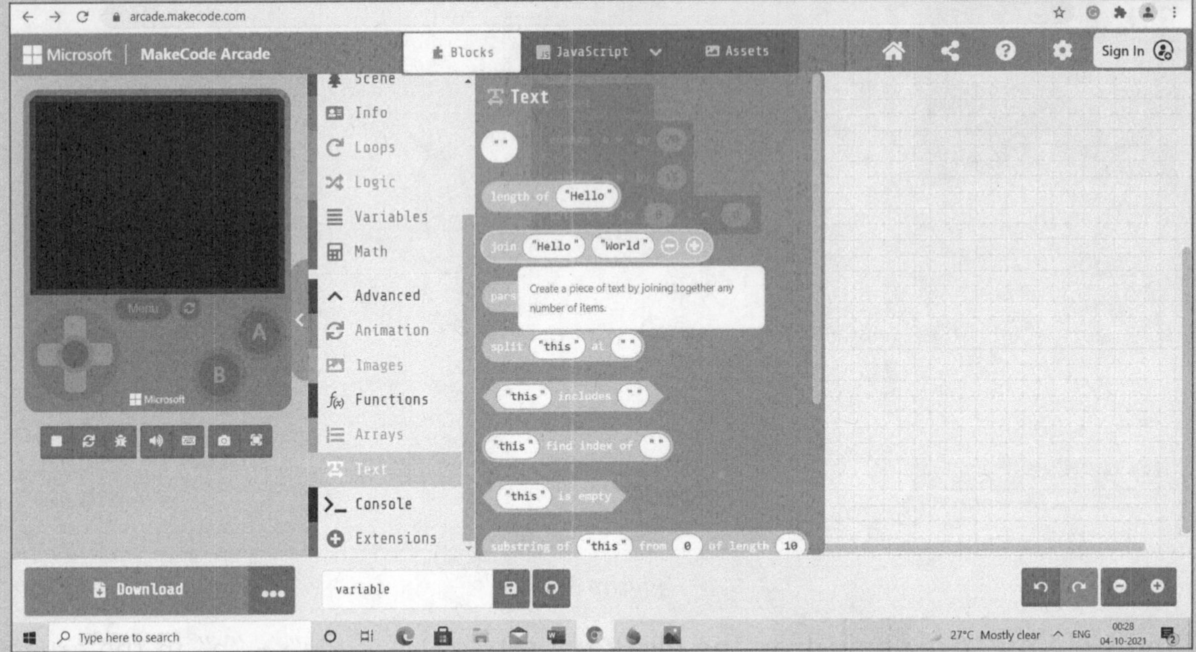

Figure 3.20

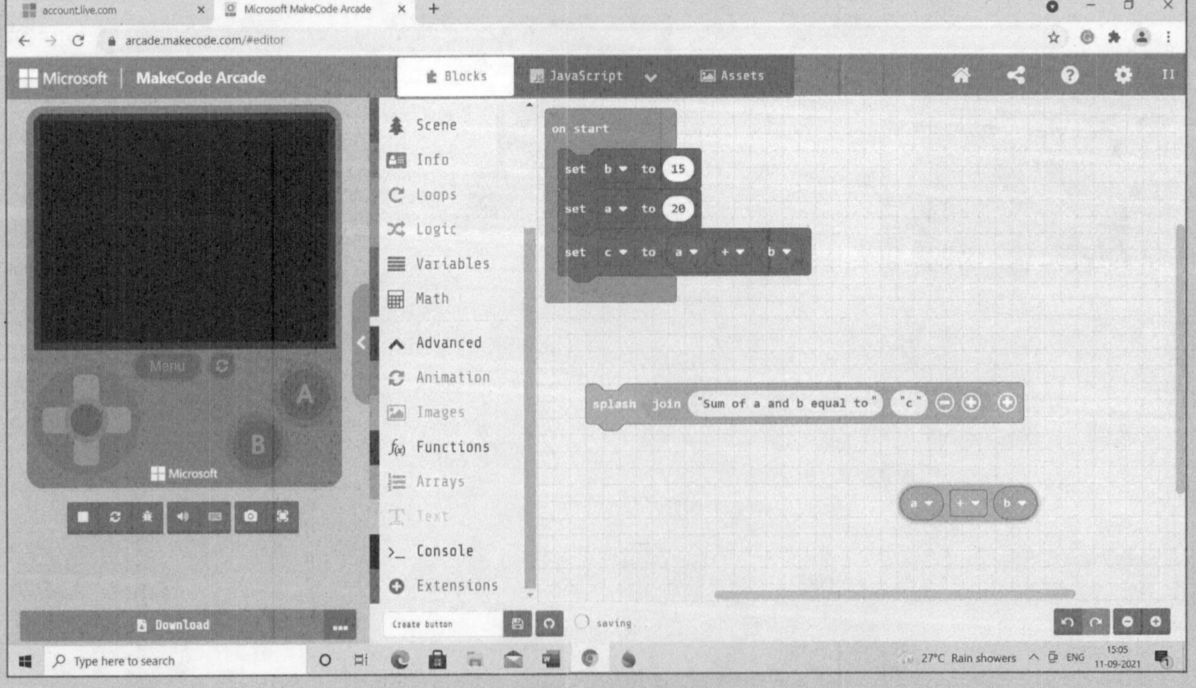

Figure 3.21

Step 14: In the 'join' operation, rename the first block as "Sum equals to" and drag and drop the variable "c" from the variables.

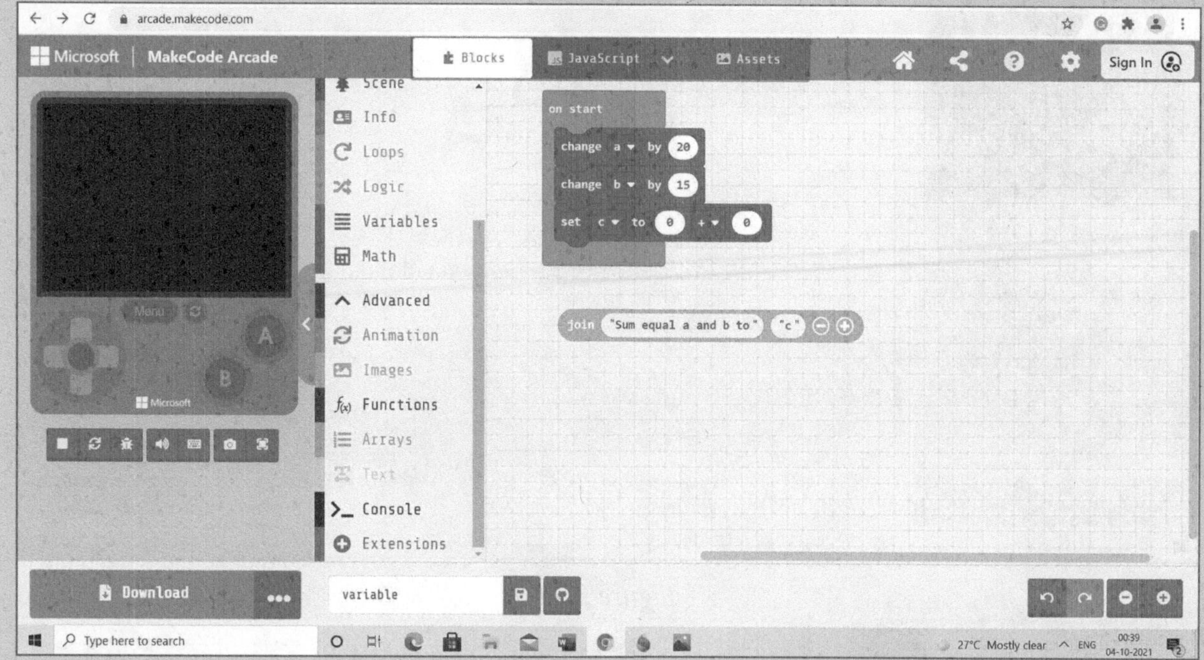

Figure 3.22

Step 15: Click on the "Games" link from the centre part of the page and click on the "Splash" block. On becoming a visible, drag and drop the "join" block into it.

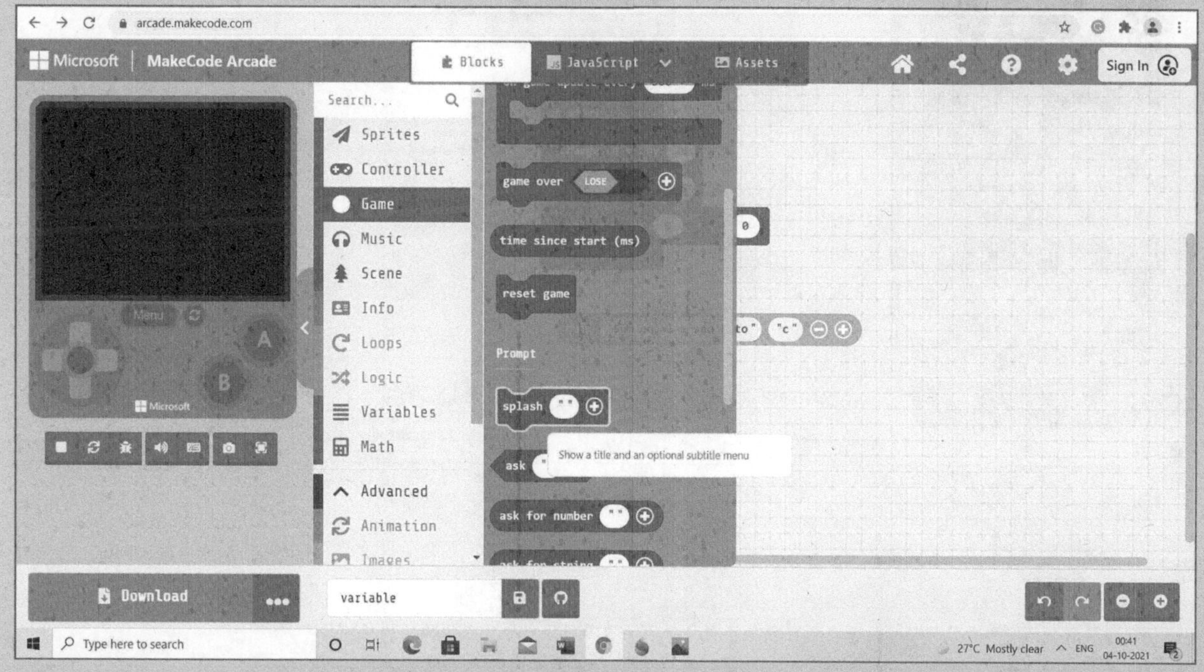

Figure 3.23

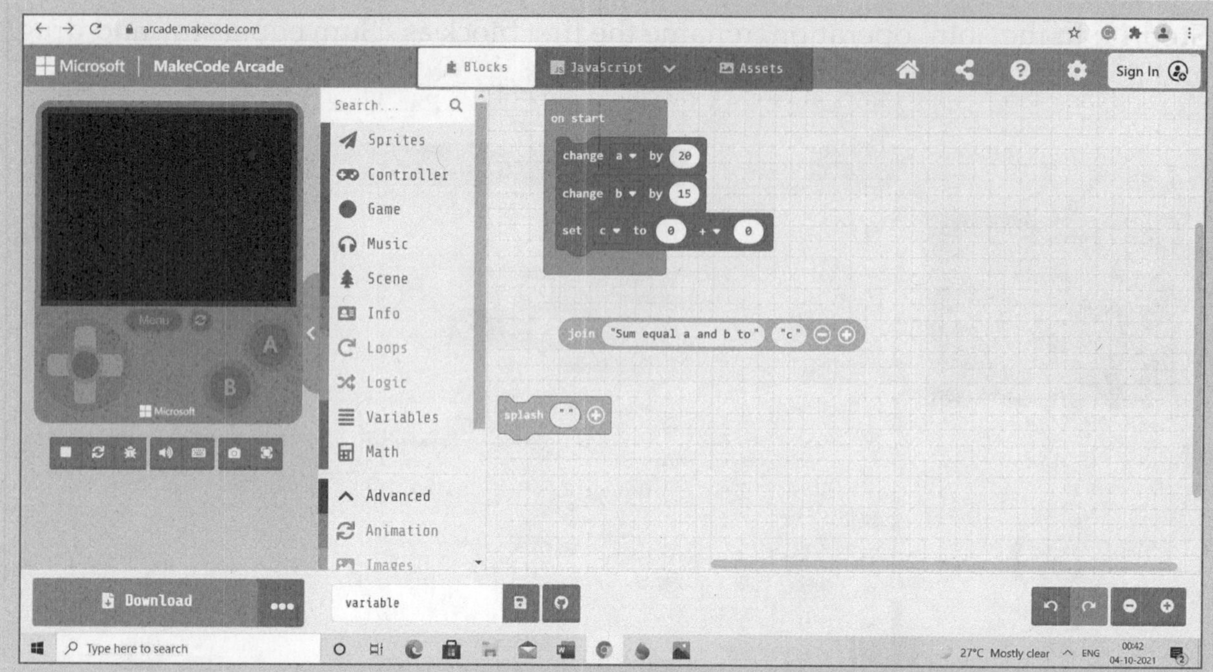

Figure 3.24

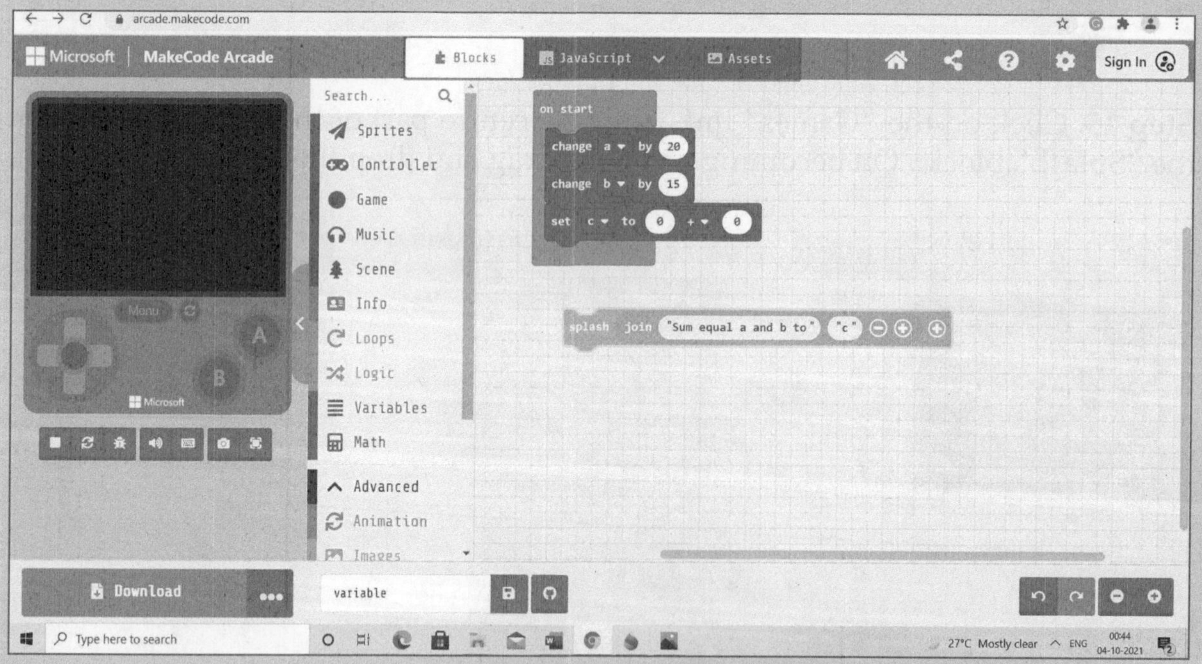

Figure 3.25

Step 16: Drag and drop the splash block into the green block below the set "c" block.

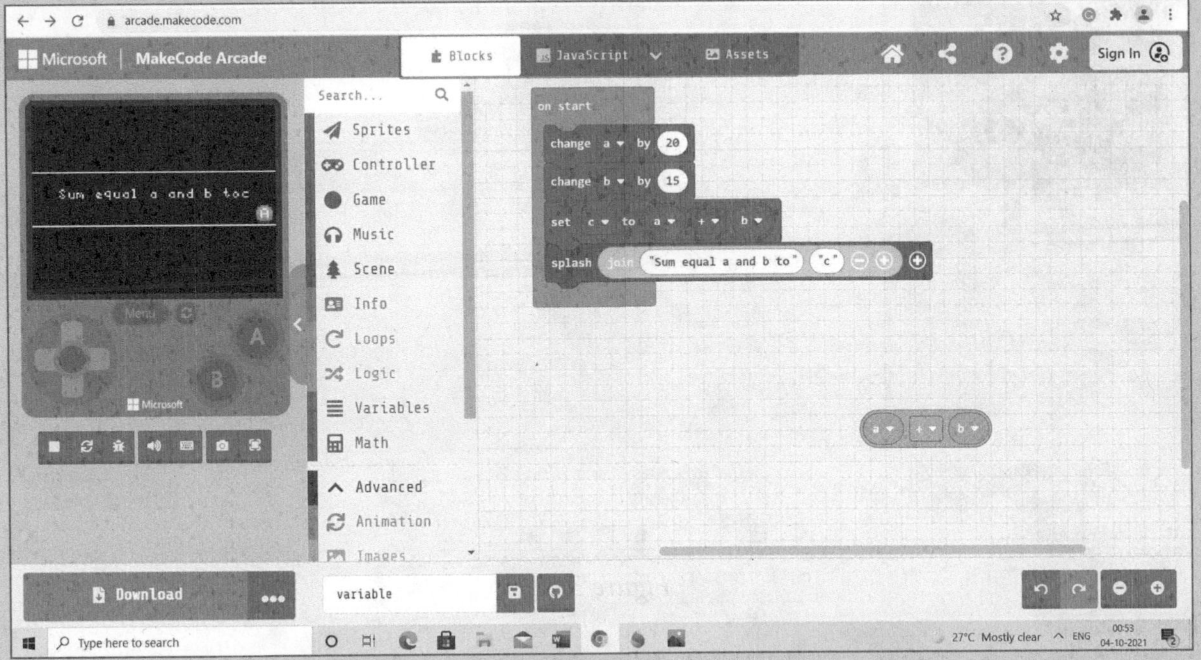

Figure 3.26

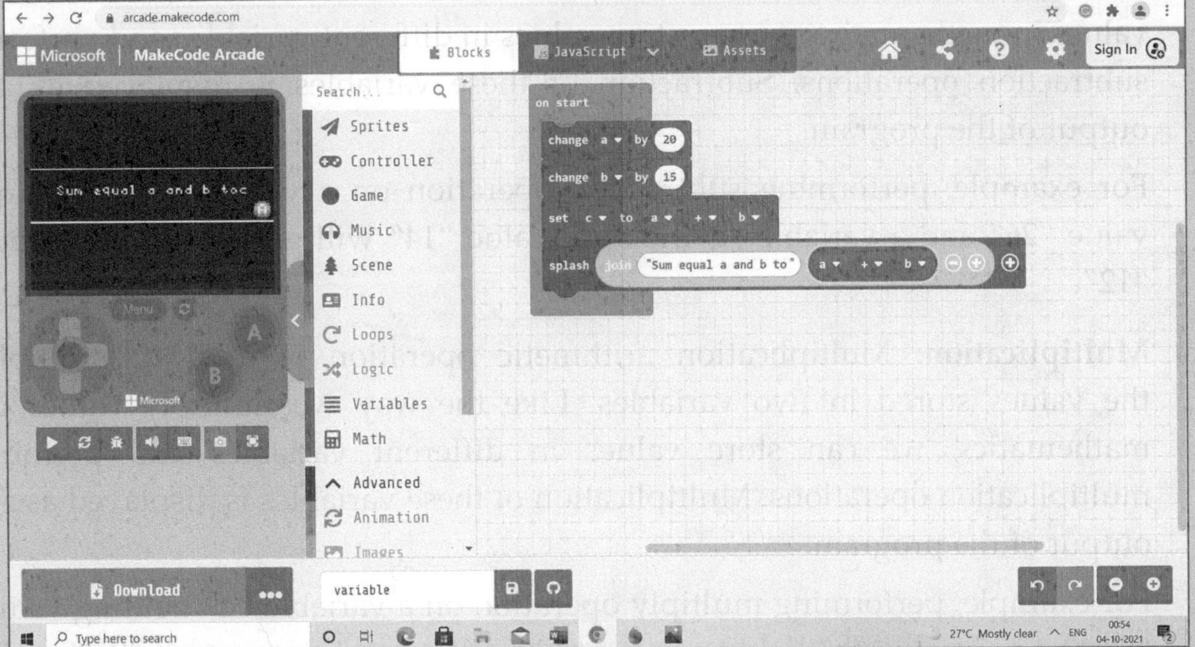

Figure 3.27

Step 17: Click the play on the button on the left-hand side of the page. You will notice that the program displays the output of the addition of two numbers, i.e., 35.

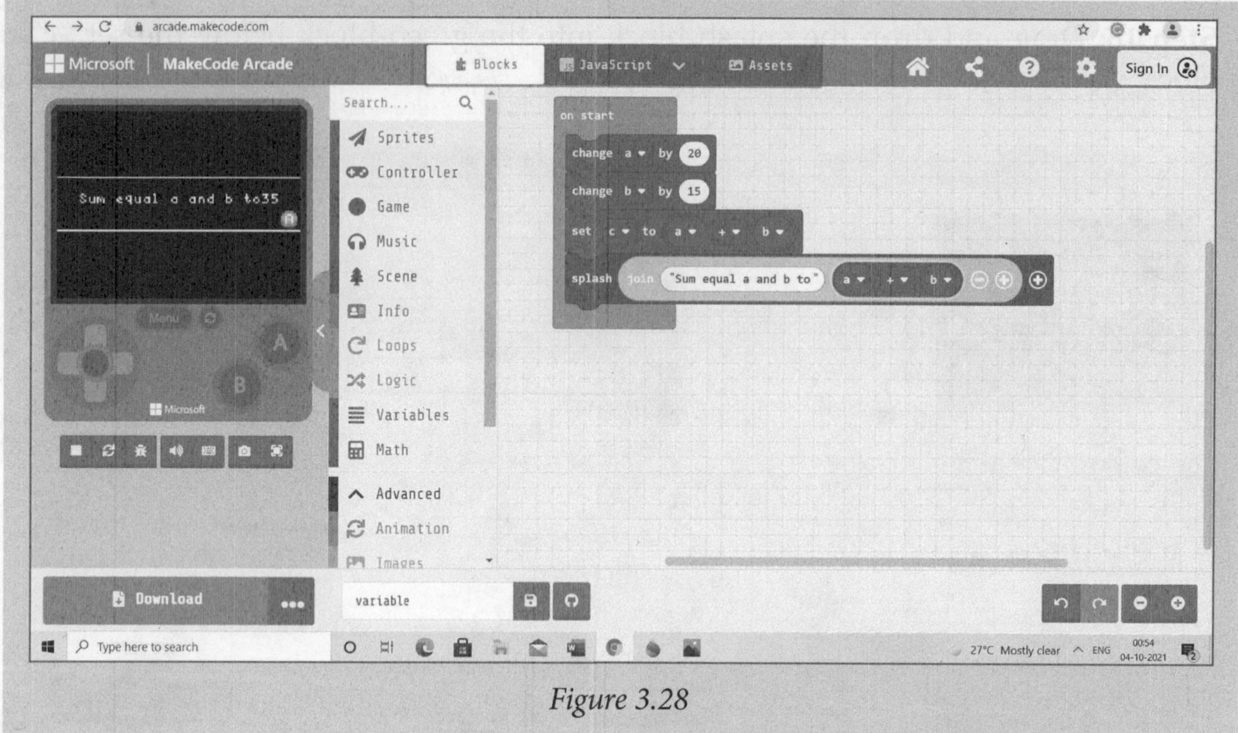

Figure 3.28

(b) Subtraction: The subtraction arithmetic operation is used to subtract the values stored in one variable from another variable. Like the way we subtract values in mathematics, we can store values in different variables and perform subtraction operations. Subtraction of these variables is displayed as an output of the program.

For example, performing subtraction operation on a variable "a" holding value "26" and a variable "b" holding value "14" will give result an output "12".

(c) Multiplication: Multiplication arithmetic operation is used to multiply the values stored in two variables. Like the way we multiply values in mathematics, we can store values in different variables and perform multiplication operations. Multiplication of these variables is displayed as an output of the program.

For example, performing multiply operation on a variable "a" holding value "8" and a variable "b" holding value "12" will result in an output "96."

(d) Division: Division arithmetic operation is used to divide the value stored in one variable by the value stored in another variable. Like the way we divide values in mathematics, we can store values in different variables and perform division operations. The division of these variables is displayed as an output of the program.

For example, performing division operation on a variable “a” holding value “12” and a variable “b” holding value “2” will result in an output “6”.

Factz Funda

Google’s Blockly is a platform that produces working code in a variety of conventional programming languages like JavaScript. This makes it possible to experiment with blocks and see the result in the desired programming language simultaneously.

(e) **Modulus (Remainder):** Modulus operator (%) calculates the remainder when two variables are divided. It should be noted that this operation can only be performed on integer and float variables in Python.

For example, performing modulus operation on a variable “a” holding value “9” and variable “b” holding value “3” will result in an output “0” as there is no remainder in this operation.

In another example, performing modulus operation on a variable “a” holding value “23” and variable “b” holding value “7” will result in an output “2” as there is a remainder of 2 in this operation.

3.5.2 Assignment Operators

An ‘Assignment operator’ is used for assigning value to a variable. Different assignment operators are shown below:

- “=”: This assignment operator is used to assign the value on the right to the left variable. *Example:* a=50
- “+=”: This operator assigns the result to the variable on the left after adding the current value of the variable on the left to the value on the right.

  Example: x += y

  It can also be written as x = x + y
- “-=”: This operator assigns the result to the variable on the left after subtracting the value of the variable on the right from the current value on the left.

  Example: x -= y

  It can also be written as x = x - y

- "*=": This operator assigns the result to the variable on the left after multiplying the current value of the variable on the left to the value on the right.
  Example: x *= y
  It can also be written as x = x * y
- "/=": This operator assigns the result to the variable on the left after dividing the current value of the variable on the left from the value on the right.
  Example: x /= y
  It can also be written as x = x / y

Details of Assignment operators are enlisted in Table 3.2.

Table 3.2 Details of assignment operators

Operator	Expression	Equivalent to
=	x=5	x=5
+=	x +=5	x = x + 5
-=	x -= 5	x = x – 5
*=	x *= 5	x = x * 5
/=	x /= 5	x = x / 5

3.5.3 Increment operator

Increment operator adds one to the value.

Example: A=8

B=A++

The output of B will be 9

(A+1) and A++ has the same meaning as A=A+1

3.5.4 Decrement operator

The decrement operator subtracts one from the value.

Example: A=8

B=A--

The output of B will be 7

(A-1)

A-- has the same meaning as A=A-1

Factz Funda

Computers use binary code to store data. This means that the computer's software is written using only 0s and 1s.

Project Time

Project 3.1

Aim: To perform a 'multiplication' operation by using Block Coding.

Learning Outcome:

- To learn how to use a mathematical operator (multiplication) in block coding.
- To learn how to use functions and variables.

Problem Statement: Using different mathematical functions is crucial during learning how to code. We will learn how to implement multiplication operations using block coding.

Solution: A multiplication arithmetic operation is used to multiply the values stored in two variables. Like the way we multiply values in mathematics, we can store values in different variables and perform a multiplication operation. The multiplication of these variables is displayed as an output of the program.

For example, performing multiply operation on a variable "a" holding value "15" and a variable "b" holding value "34" will result in an output "510". We will use variables to solve such type of problems. Use the following steps to solve the problem:

Step1: Open the MakeCode arcade home screen.

Figure 3.29

Step 2: Click on "New Project," give a name to the project "Arithmetic Operations," and click on the "'create" button.

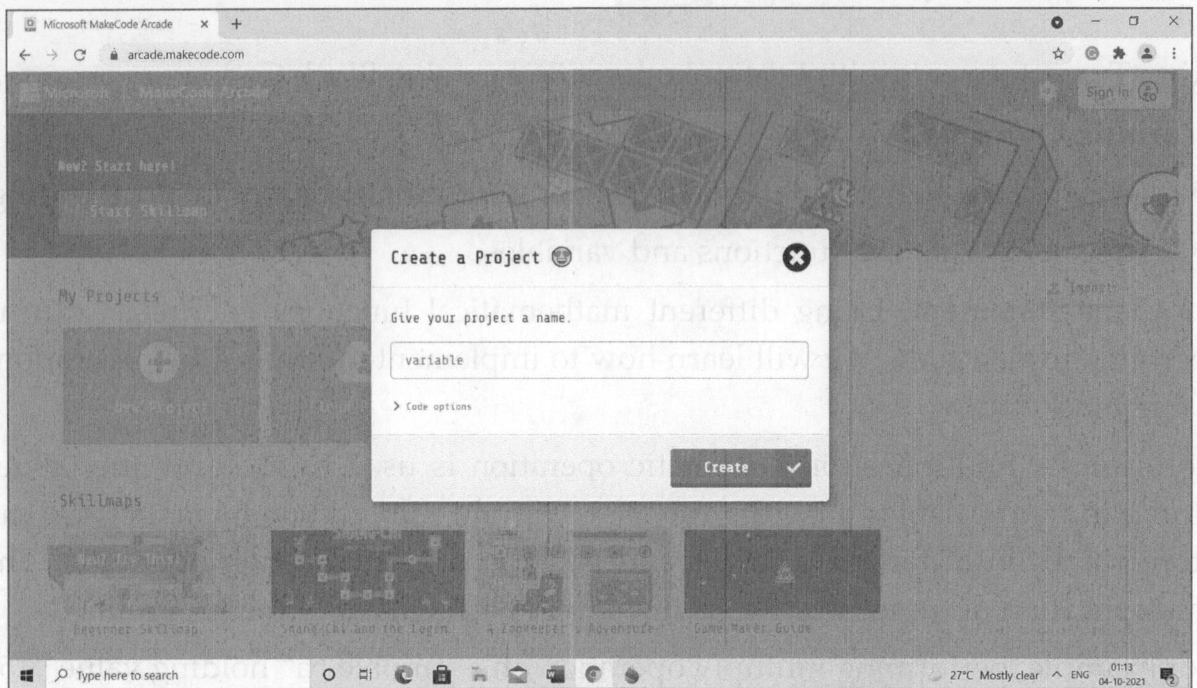

Figure 3.30

Step 3: From the list in the centre of the page, click on "Variables" and then click on "Make a Variable."

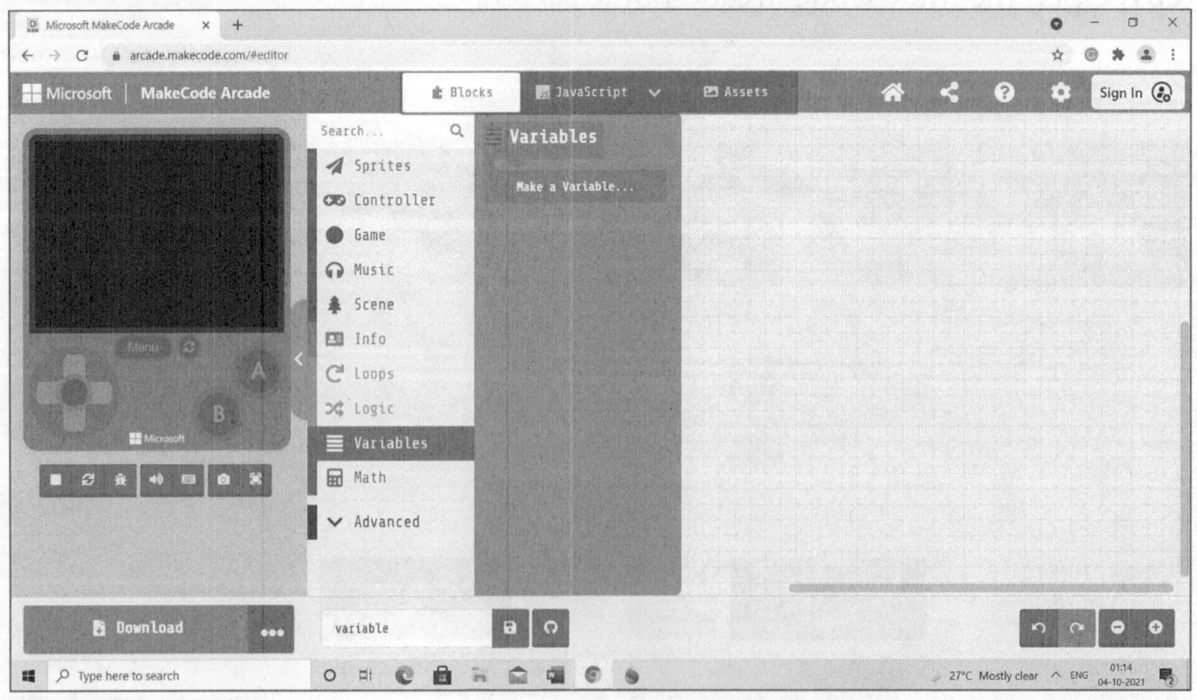

Figure 3.31

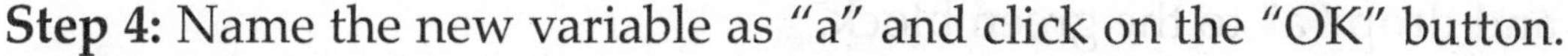

Step 4: Name the new variable as "a" and click on the "OK" button.

Figure 3.32

Step 5: Click on the value of "a" and change to the desired value. In this case, we are taking it as "34".

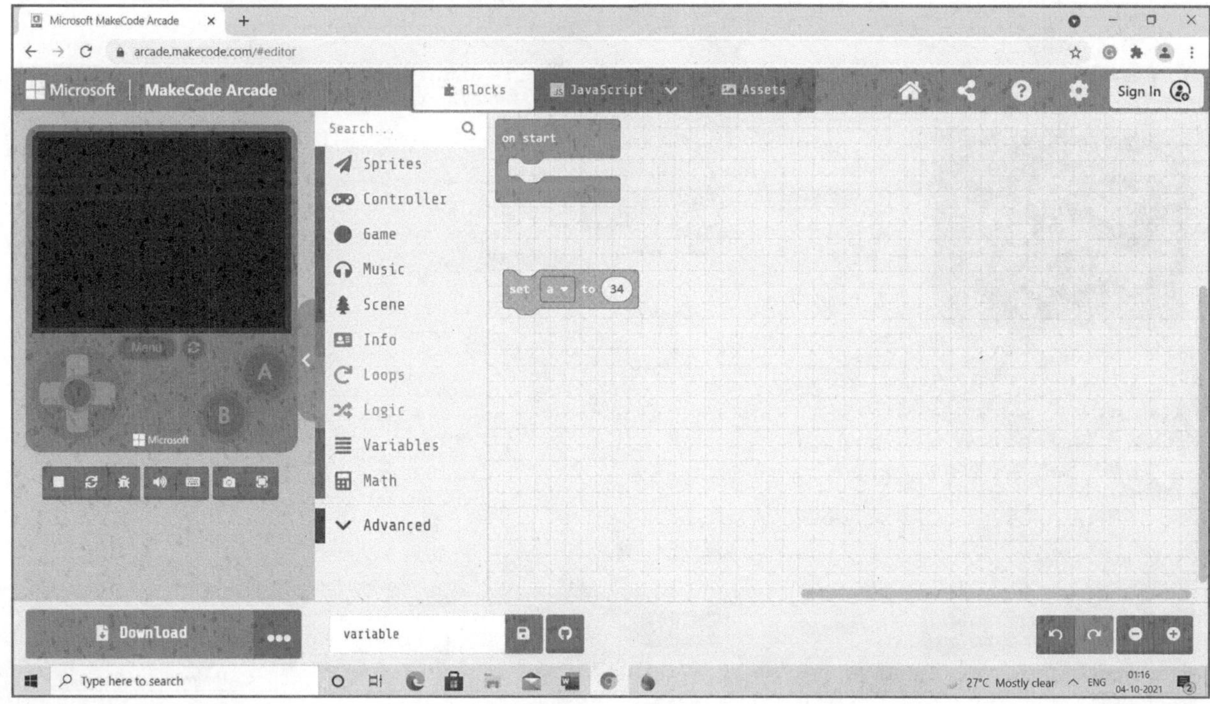

Figure 3.33

Step 6: Drag and drop "a" to the green block.

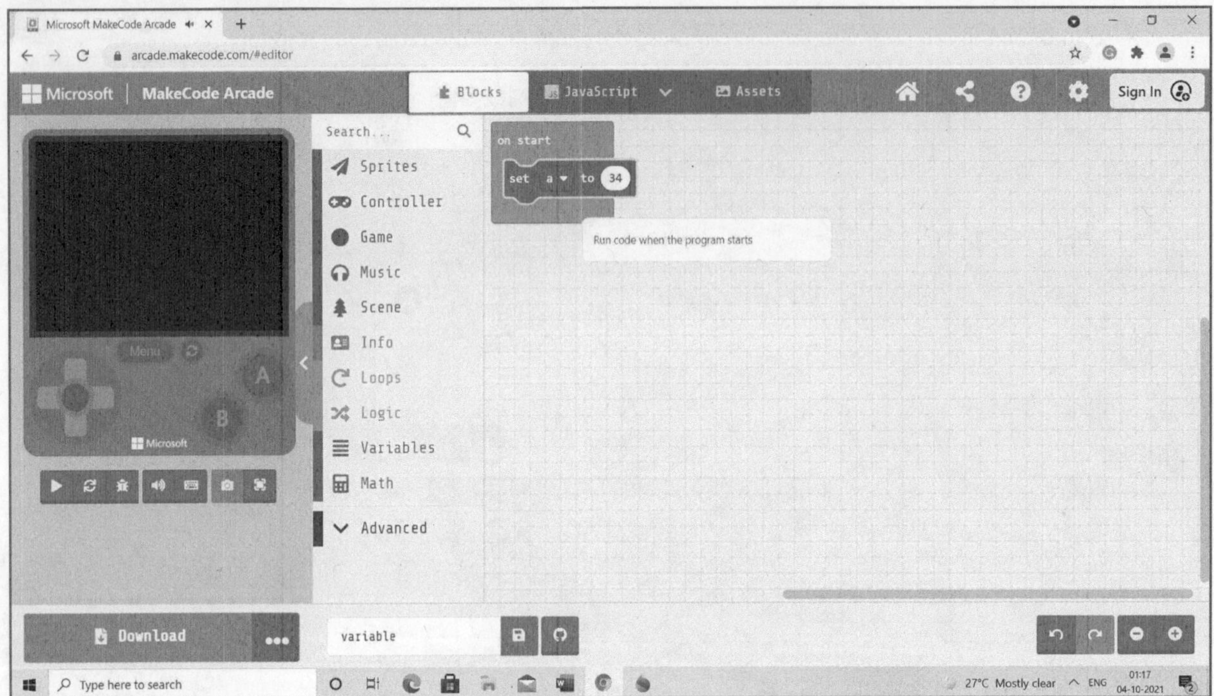

Figure 3.34

Step 7: Similarly, make another variable "b" and assign it a value "25," and drag and drop it on the green block.

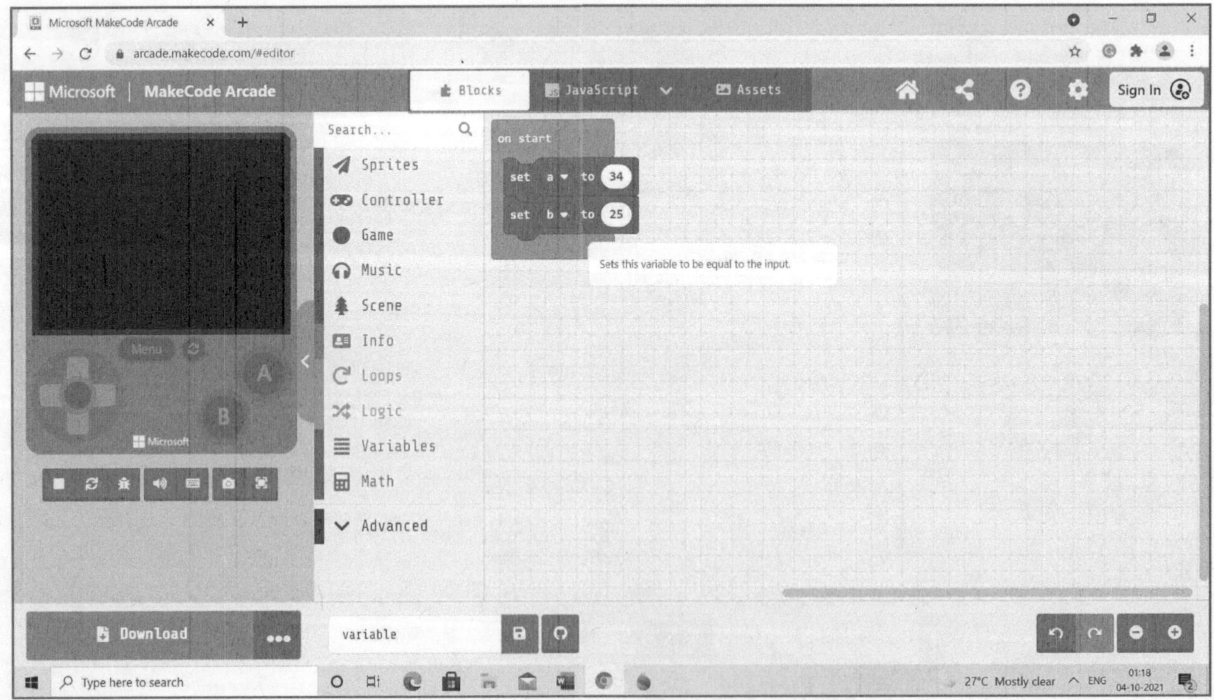

Figure 3.35

Step 8: Now, click on the "Math" link from the centre of the page and click on multiplication operation.

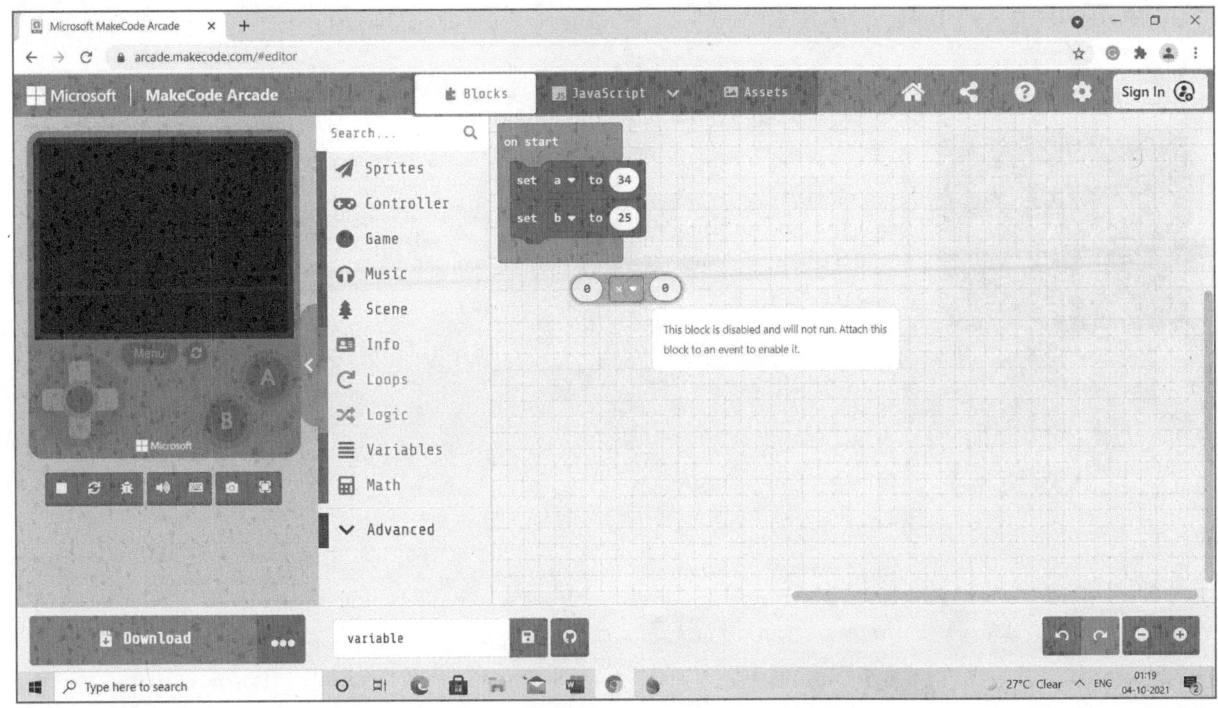

Figure 3.36

Step 9: Now, click on the "Variables" link from the centre of the page and drag and drop variables "a" and "b" in the multiplication box as seen in the screenshot.

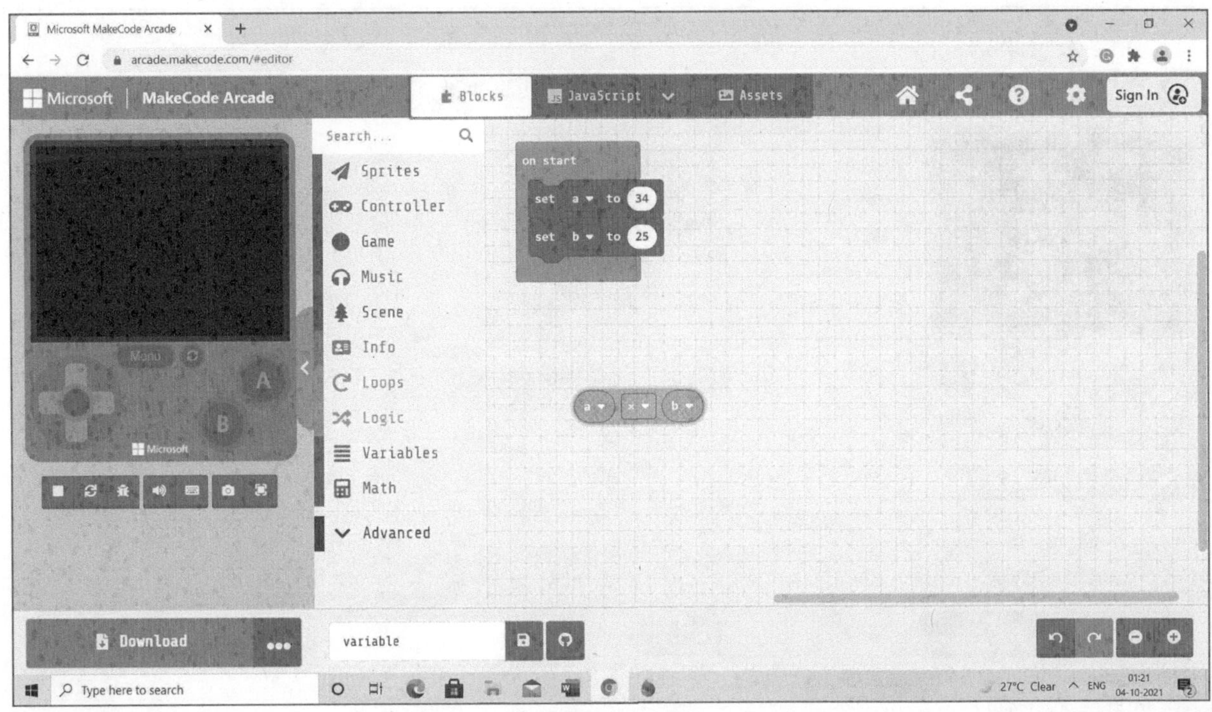

Figure 3.37

Step 10: Like the way we had created variables a and b, now create variable c. Drag and drop block of variable c to in the play area.

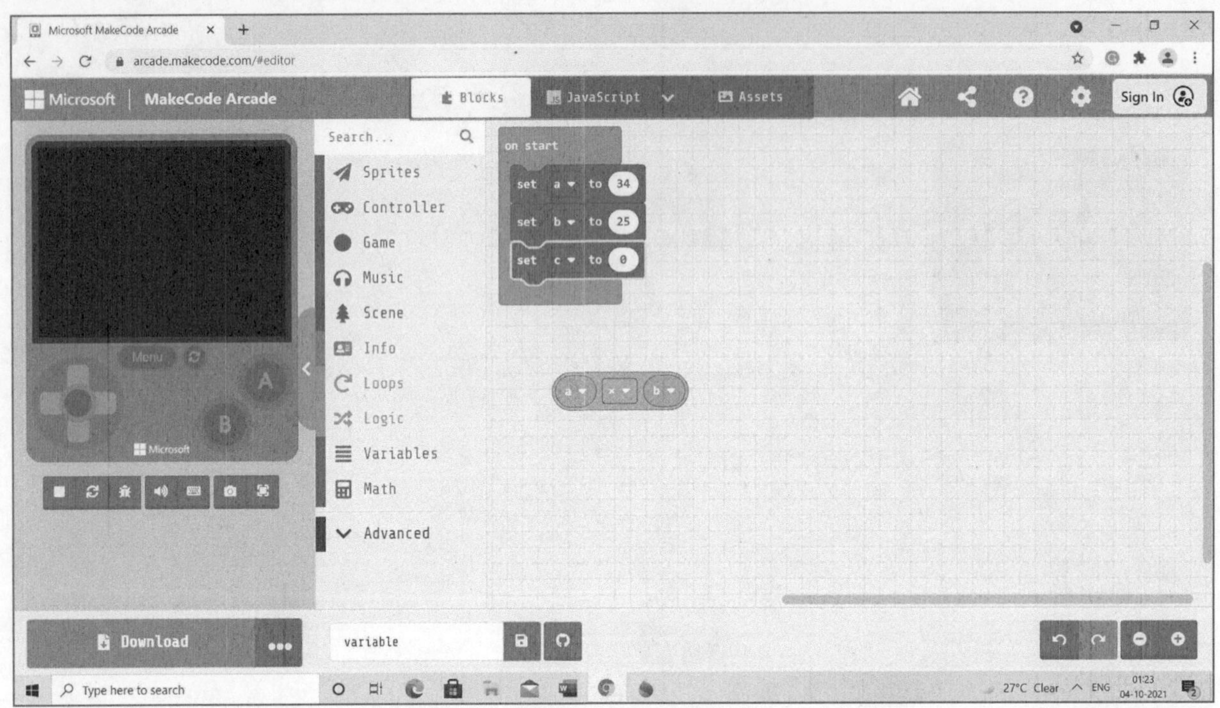

Figure 3.38

Step 11: Now, drag and drop multiplication block in the set "c" to block as seen in the screenshot.

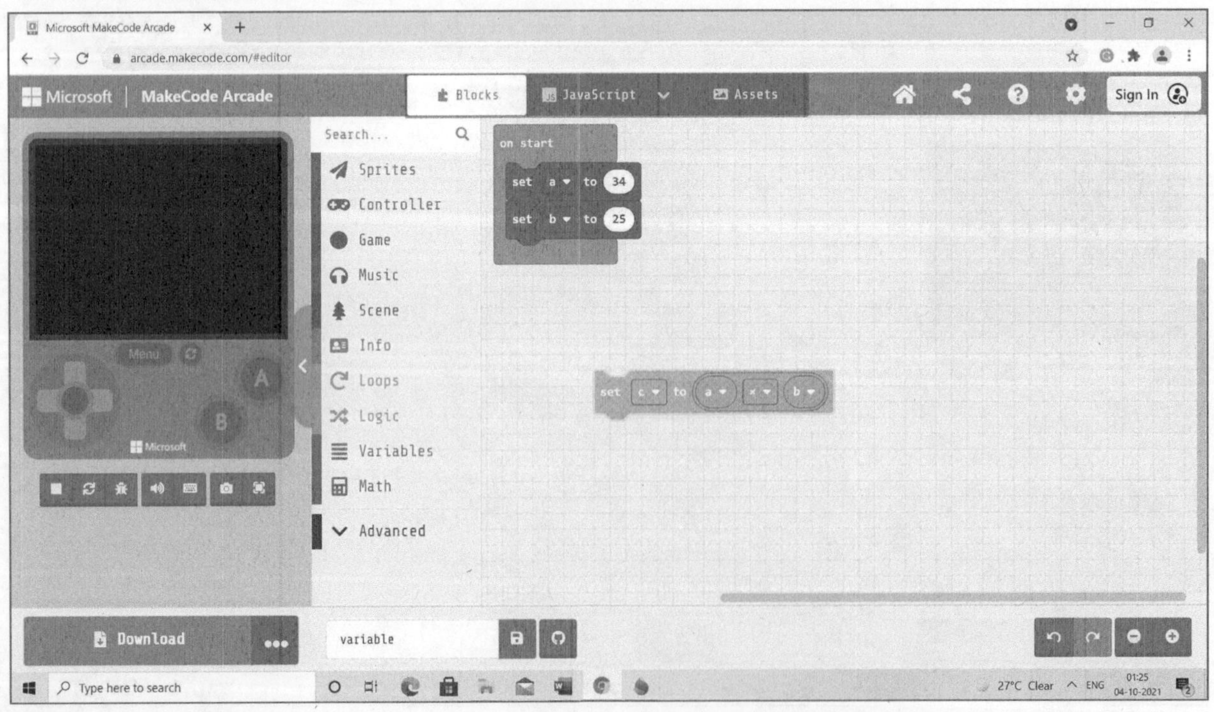

Figure 3.39

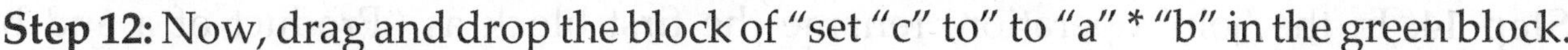

Step 12: Now, drag and drop the block of "set "c" to" to "a" * "b" in the green block.

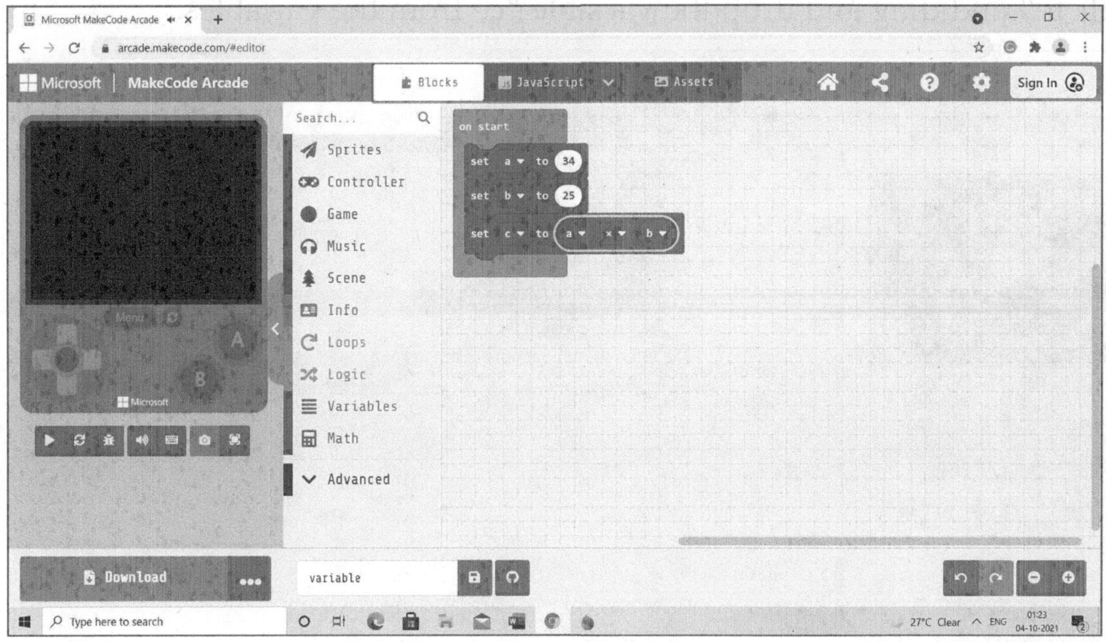

Figure 3.40

Step 13: We have created the variables and assigned them the values, and then created a third variable, "c," which will have the output of multiplication of "a" and "b." Now, we will execute the program. For this, click on the "Advanced " link from the centre part of the page and then click on the "Text" link to select the "Join" operation from the list.

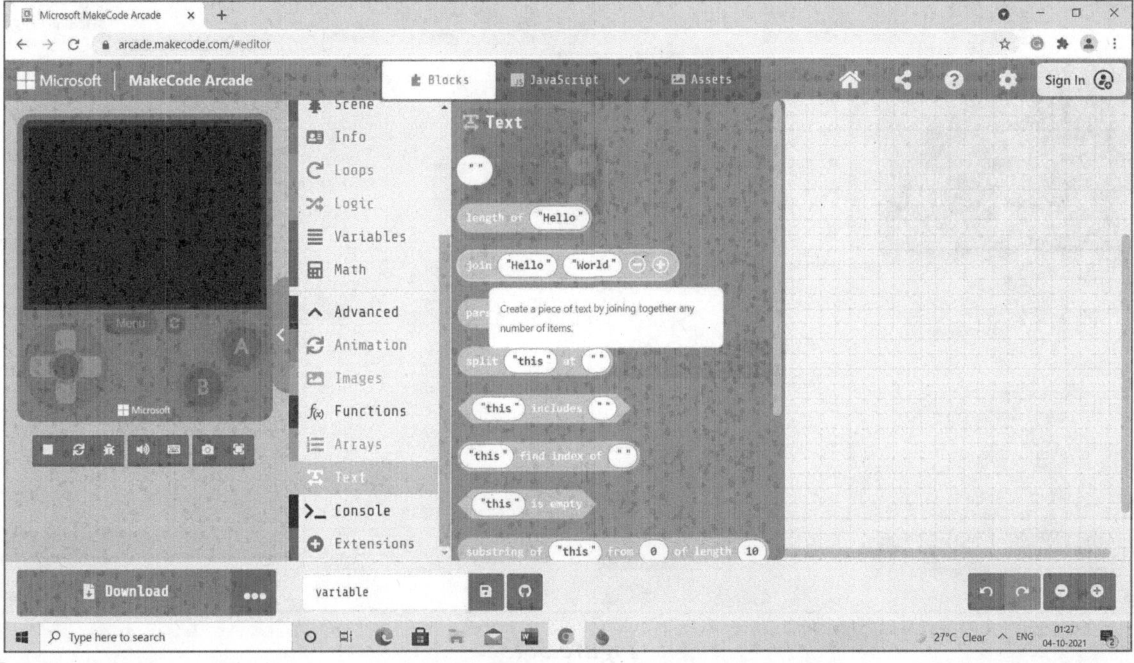

Figure 3.41

Step 14: In the 'join' operation, rename the first block as "Product of a and b equals to" and drag and drop the variable "c" from the variables.

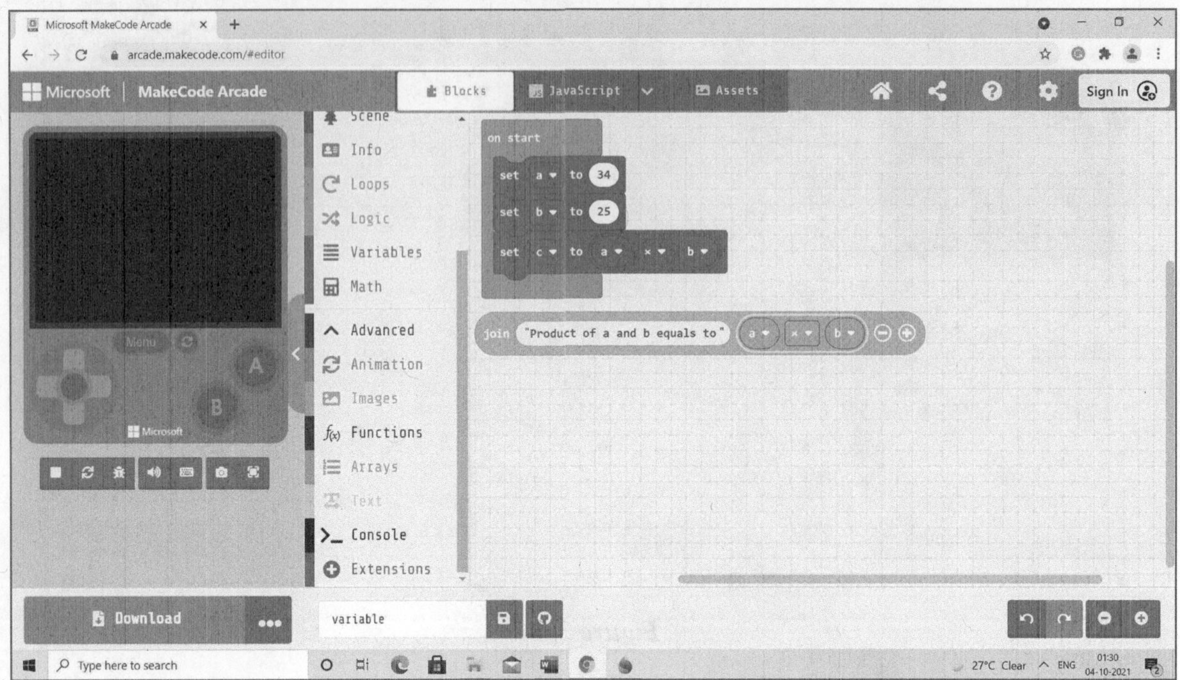

Figure 3.42

Step 15: Click on the "Games" link from the centre part of the page and click on the "Splash" block. On becoming a visible, drag and drop the "join" block into it.

Figure 3.43

Step 16: Drag and drop the splash block into the green block below the set "c" block.

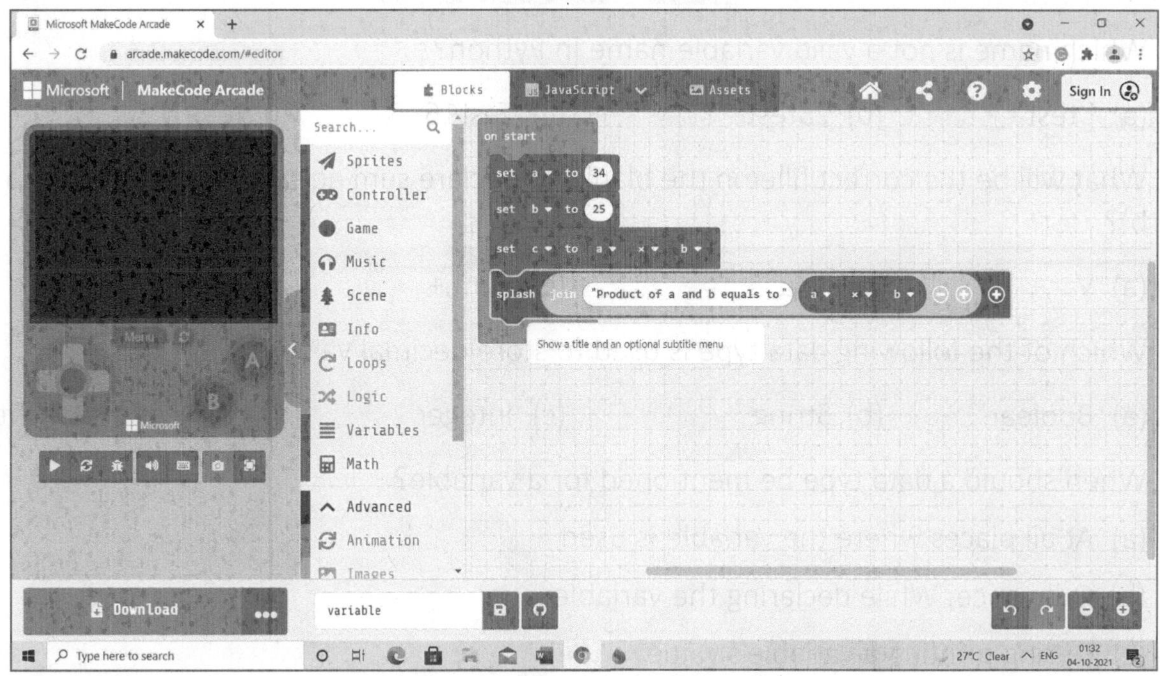

Figure 3.44

Step 17: Click the play on the button on the left-hand side of the page. You will notice that the program displays the output of multiplication of two numbers, i.e., 850.

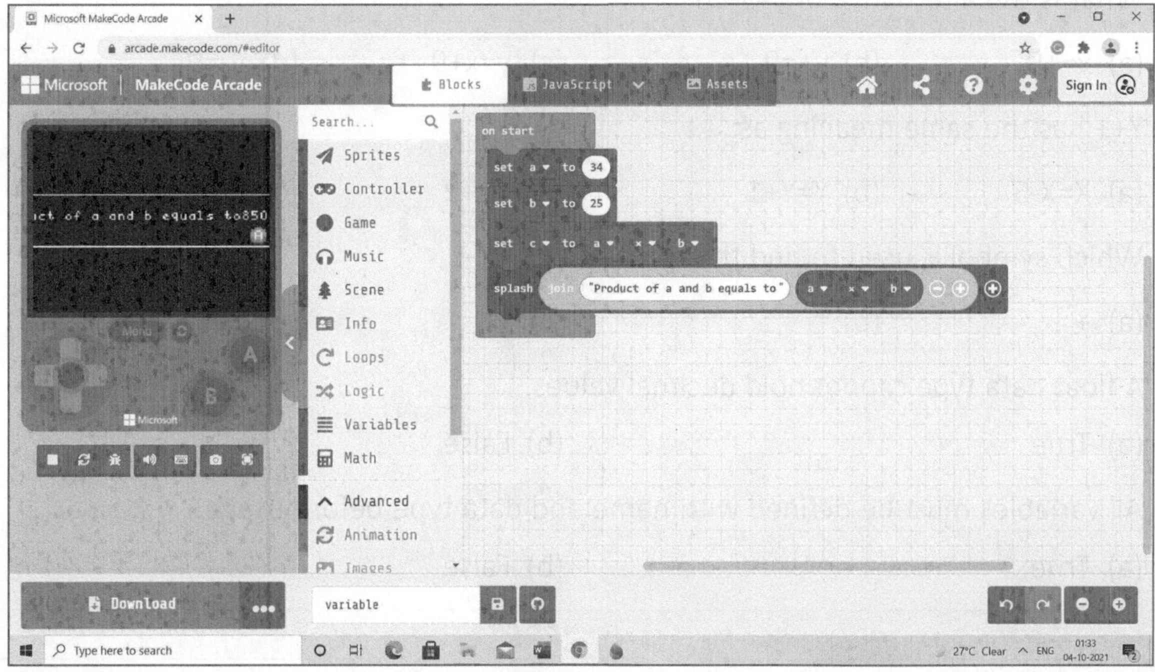

Figure 3.45.

1. Which name is not a valid variable name in Python?

   (a) _test (b) 23test (c) Test16 (d) Test_4

2. What will be the correct filler in the blanks to declare sum equal to a + b (int ..... = a .... b)?

   (a) Var,+ (b) Add,- (c) Sum,+ (d) Bool,+

3. Which of the following data type is used to store decimal values?

   (a) Boolean (b) String (c) Integer (d) None of the above

4. When should a data type be mentioned for a variable?

   (a) At all places where the variable is used

   (b) Only once; While declaring the variable

   (c) During printing a variable's value;

   (d) While entering variable's value;

5. Which symbol is used to multiply variables?

   (a) + (b) % (c) * (d) x

6. What is the alternative of y=y+9?

   (a) x=+9 (b) y+=9 (c) y=x+9 (d) y-=9

7. Y++ has the same meaning as:

   (a) X=X-5 (b) Y=Y+1 (c) X=+2 (d) Y-=6

8. Which symbol is used to find the remainder?

   (a) + (b) * (c) % (d) x

9. A float data type cannot hold decimal values.

   (a) True (b) False

10. All variables must be defined with name and data type before usage.

    (a) True (b) False

ANSWERS									
1. (b)	2. (c)	3. (d)	4. (b)	5. (c)	6. (b)	7. (b)	8. (c)	9. (b)	10. (a)

SUMMARY

- A variable is defined as a named location that is used to store data in the memory of the computer.
- The variable is taken as a container (like envelope or bucket) holding data that can be changed later throughout programming.
- Scope of a variable normally refers to the part of the code where the variable can be used.
- The name which is assigned to a variable, acts as an identifier for that variable.
- In programming, a user is not allowed to use the same name of a variable more than once.
- Naming variables make it easier to call them while performing operations.
- The name of a variable also suggests what information the variable contains.
- Data type identifies the type of data that the declared variable can hold.
- The declaration of a variable in a program contains two components – the name of the variable and its type.
- Integer data type variables store integer values only. They store whole numbers which have zero, positive and negative values but not decimal values.
- If a user tries to create an integer variable and assign it a non-integer value, the program returns an error.
- Variables of the integer data type are only capable of holding single values.
- Floating-point numbers are used to store decimal values.
- There is another type of floating-point number known as a "double" data type, which is used to store even bigger values.
- Character type variables are used to store character values.
- Syntax of declaring a character variable is specific to the programming language that you are using.
- Any character value can be declared as a 'char' variable.
- The String data type stores value in a sequence of characters, i.e., in String format.
- Boolean Data Type stores values in Boolean type only, i.e., "true" or "false."
- Boolean is a subtype of integer data type that stores true and false where true means non-zero and false means zero.
- Operators are special symbols that represent computation. They are applied to operand(s), which can be values or variables.
- Operators, when applied to operands, form an expression.

- An arithmetic operation combines two or more numeric expressions using the Arithmetic Operators to form a resulting numeric expression.
- An 'Assignment operator' is used to assigning value to a variable.

PRACTICE TIME

(A) True/False Type Questions

1. The variable is assumed as a container (like envelope or bucket) holding data that can be changed later throughout programming.
2. Scope of a variable normally refers to the part of the code where the variable can be used.
3. In programming, a user is allowed to use the same name of a variable more than once.
4. Naming variables make it difficult to call them while performing operations.
5. The name of a variable also suggests what information the variable contains.
6. The declaration of a variable in a program contains two components – the name of the variable and its type.
7. Boolean data type stores whole numbers which have zero, positive and negative values but not decimal values.
8. If a user tries to create an integer variable and assign it a non-integer value, the program returns an error.
9. Variables of the integer data type are only capable of holding single values.
10. The floating-point number, known as the "double" data type, is used to store bigger values.

ANSWERS					
1. T	2. T	3. F (not allowed)	4. F (easier)	5. T	6. T
7. F (Integer)	8. T	9. T	10. T		

(B) Fill in the blanks

1. A ____________ is a named location that is used to store data in the memory of the computer.
2. The name assigned to a variable acts as an ____________ for that variable.
3. ____________ type variables are used to store character values.
4. ____________ identifies what the type of data that the declared variable can hold.

5. Integer data type variables store ____________ values only.
6. ____________ numbers are used to store decimal values.
7. The ____________ data type stores value in a sequence of characters, i.e., in String format.
8. ____________ Data Type stores values in Boolean type only, i.e., "true" or "false."
9. ____________ are special symbols that represent computation. They are applied to operand(s), which can be values or variables.
10. ____________ operator is used to assigning value to a variable.

ANSWERS				
1. variable	2. identifier	3. Character	4. Data type	5. integer
6. Floating-point	7. String	8. Boolean	9. Operators	10. Assignment

(C) Very Short Answers Questions

1. Define variables in programming.
2. Can we declare two variables in a program with the same name?
3. Name a data type that can store exponential values.
4. What do you mean by the 'scope of a variable'?
5. What is Boolean data type?

(D) Short Answer Questions

1. What do you mean by string data type? Give two examples.
2. Name the common Data Types in programming.
3. Write the pseudocode to perform an addition operation on two variables in a program.
4. Define and illustrate floating data types.
5. Define operators and operands.

(E) High Order Thinking Skill Questions (HOTS)

1. Why is naming to variables done?
2. Create a flowchart to perform the different mathematical operations (Multiplication and Division) on two variables.

(F) Projects

1. Create a flowchart to perform different mathematical operations (Multiplication, Subtraction, Addition, Division) on two or more variables.

2. Create a project in https://arcade.makecode.com/ to perform a Modulus operation on two variables in a program.
3. Using block coding, create your normal school day (Monday to Friday) by using the following guidelines:

   Getting ready for school

   - Look at your timetable and pack your school bag accordingly.
   - If Physical Education (PE) is there, then packing your PE uniform and shoes

   At school

   - Attend the morning session with subjects Math, English, and science
   - A decision on what to play during recess
   - Attend the afternoon session subjects
   - Lunch Break
   - PE Class

   After reaching home

   - Have snacks
   - Depending on the day, choose the class you must attend.

   (Monday-Judo, Tuesday-Aeromodeling, Wednesday-Swimming, Thursday-Chess, Friday-Dance, Saturday-Vedic Maths)

   (Use variables to define the class you have to attend)

Control with Conditionals

Structure

In this chapter, you will learn:

- The conditions and how to apply them in real life?
- The different types of operators
- Combining multiple operators
- Logical operators- AND, OR, NOT.
- Applying logical operations in block coding

INTRODUCTION

Humans make so many decisions in their daily lives. Some decisions are taken based on some conditions. For example, if there is no rain, then I will go to the market. Here, a condition of "no rain" is applied for going to market. In programming, decision-making or branching statements are used to select one path based on the result of the evaluated expression. It is also called a control statement because it controls the flow of execution of a program. If and if-else statements are used for decision-making statements.

In this chapter, we shall study different types of operators, combining multiple operators, Logical operators and applying logical operations in block coding.

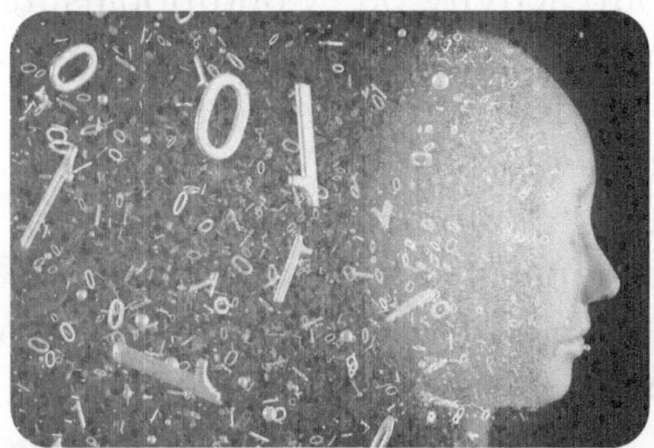

Figure 4.1

Learning Objectives:

At the end of this chapter, you will be able to:

- Have an understanding of the AND, OR, NOT logical operators.
- Combine different logical operators.
- Understand how to apply logical operators in block coding.
- Understand nested conditional statements in block coding.

4.1 CONDITIONALS AND HOW TO APPLY THEM IN REAL LIFE?

We make many decisions in our daily lives. Some decisions are based on some conditions in real life. Consider the following statements:

- If papaji gives me Rs fifty as pocket money, I will enjoy ice cream today.
- If no invitation card is received, we will not attend the party.
- If there is a crowd on the bus, we will travel by using a taxi.
- If you promise to provide me financial help, then only I will start my business.
- If railway ticket cum reservation is available, then I will travel by train, else I will go by air.
- When both Ramesh and Sunita say yes, then our family will accompany them for a picnic.
- If there is no rain, and if there is no traffic jam, then we will go to Shoprix Mall to enjoy a film show.
- Either Sugandha or Sneha will attend the school; then, the farewell party will begin.

Activity 4.1

Group Discussion and Oral Presentation

- Participate in the group activity on "Conditionals in our real-life."
- The students will be distributed in four groups randomly without gender bias.
- Each group will discuss the topic and will frame at least ten control/conditional statements from real life.

Figure 4.2

- Two representatives from each group (one boy and one girl) will present the list before the full class.

4.2 OPERATORS

An operator is a symbol that performs mathematical operations on variables or on values. The Operators operate on operands (values) and return a result.

There are seven types of operators:

- Arithmetic Operators
- Relational Operators
- Assignment Operators
- Logical Operators
- Membership Operators
- Identity Operators
- Bitwise Operators

4.2.1 Arithmetic Operators

Arithmetic operators are the most common. There are seven arithmetic operators for different mathematical operations. They are:

- + (Addition)
- -(Subtraction)
- *(Multiplication)
- / (Division)
- ** (Exponentiation)
- // (Floor division)
- % (Modulus)

4.2.2 Relational Operators

Relational operators are also called comparison operators, and they compare values.

There are 6 relational operators:

- > (Greater than)
- < (Less than)
- == (Equal to)
- != (Not equal to)
- >= (Greater than or equal to)
- <= (Less than or equal to)

4.2.3 Assignment Operators

Assignment operators perform an operation and assign a value. There are eight assignment operators:

- = (Assign)
- += (Add and assign)
- -= (Subtract and assign)
- *= (Multiply and assign)
- /= (Divide and assign)
- %= (Modulus and assign)
- **= (Exponentiation and assign)
- //= (Floor-divide and assign)

4.2.4 Logical Operators

Logical Operators can combine conditions. There are three logical operators:

❖ And (Logical And) ❖ Or (Logical Or) ❖ Not (Logical Not)

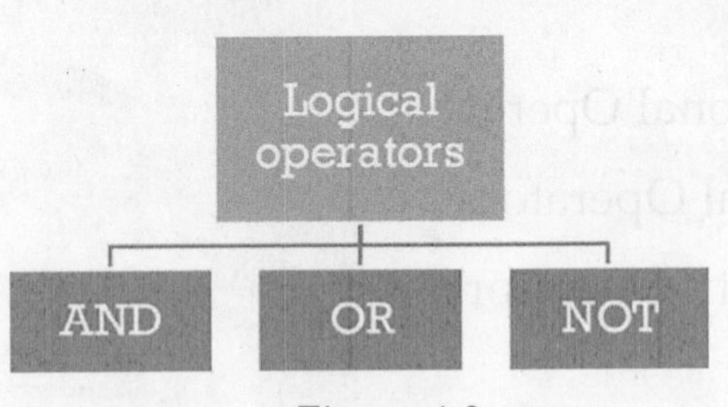

Figure 4.3

Factz Funda

Conditional statements execute in a sequence when there is no condition around the statements.

4.2.5 Membership Operators

Membership operators check whether a value is in another value or not. There are two membership operators:

❖ in ❖ not in

4.2.6 Identity Operators

Identity operators check whether two values are identical or not. There are two identity operators :

❖ is ❖ is not

4.2.7 Bitwise Operators

Bitwise operators operate on values bit by bit. There are six bitwise operators:

❖ & (Bitwise and)

❖ | (Bitwise or)

❖ ^ (Bitwise xor)

❖ ~ (Bitwise 1′s complement)

❖ << (Bitwise left-shift)

❖ >> (Bitwise right-shift)

Factz Funda

Block coding is a process used in computer programming where text-based software codes change to a visual block format to create characters, animated games, stories, etc.

4.3 ARRANGING BLOCKS

In the figure 4.4, what are you seeing?

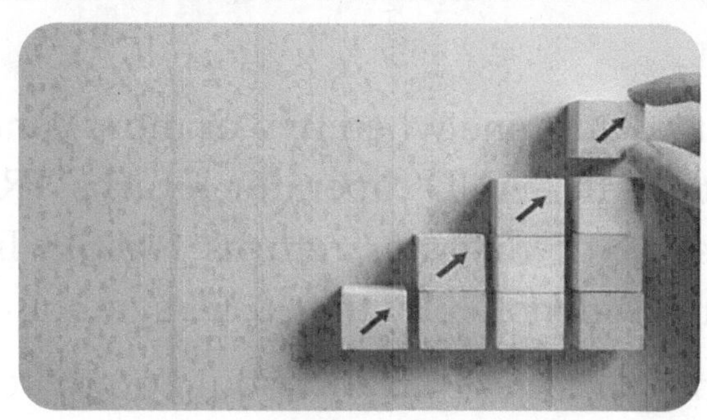

Figure 4.4

Yes, you see several blocks arranged in a specific order. Every time we place a new block in block coding, we apply logic to build a diagonal line with blocks marked with arrows. This logic in coding terms is called conditions. Similarly, every day we make many decisions depending on some situations. For example, when it is summer outside, we wear light clothes otherwise, we don't.

4.4 LOGICAL OPERATORS

Logical operators are called fundamental blocks that can be used to build a decision-making capability in the code. In the earlier chapters, we discussed how to handle decisions in a flow chart. Now, we shall learn how to implement it in the code. We can do things with conditions in our programs using 'if' statements or 'if else' statements combined with logical operators. Logical operators perform like Boolean variables and return either TRUE or FALSE.

They can combine conditions. There are three logical operators:

- And (Logical and)
- Or (Logical or)
- Not (Logical not)

Table 4.1 Details of logical operators

Operator	Meaning	Expression	Result
and	And operator	True and True	True
		True and False	False
or	Or operator	True or False	True
		False or False	False
not	Not Operator	not False	True
		not True	False

4.4.1 And operator

AND operator is used to determine when two or more conditions are true. When all the conditions are true, the 'AND' operator returns TRUE. When any one of the conditions fail, the 'AND' operator returns FALSE. In some programming languages AND operator is denoted by the "&&" symbol.

For example: Aniket and her sister Shivani should go to bed only after they have completed their homework and the time is past 10 PM. Here, when we derive the logical operation from this scenario, we will have the following conditions:

Factz Funda

The logical 'And' operator returns True if both values are True. Otherwise, it returns False.

Condition 1: Have they completed homework?

Condition 2: Is the time past 10 PM?

And the decision we are deriving is:

Decision: Should they go to bed?

Based on this, we will have the following pseudo-code:

```
IF (Homework completed) AND (Time is past 10 PM)
THEN
    Go to bed
ELSE
    Do not go to bed
END
```

The different combinations possible with the above pseudo-code are shown in Table 4.2.

Table 4.2 Different possibilities

Condition 1	Condition 2	Decision
Have you completed homework?	Is the time past 10 PM?	Should you go to bed?
Yes	Yes	Yes
No	Yes	No
Yes	No	No
No	No	No

After seeing this example, let us now find out how this is different from the OR operator.

Factz Funda

Conditional Statements programming is used to make decisions based on the conditions.

4.4.2 OR OPERATOR

The OR operator is used to determine if either one of two or more conditions is TRUE. When any one of the conditions is true, the OR operator returns TRUE. If all the conditions fail, the OR operator simply returns FALSE. In some programming languages, OR operator is denoted by the "||" symbol.

Factz Funda

The logical 'or' operator returns True when even one value is True. It returns False when both values are False.

For example, We should carry an umbrella either it is sunny, or it is raining. Otherwise, we should not carry it. If we want to derive the logical operation from this scenario, we will have the following conditions:

Condition 1: Is it sunny outside?

Condition 2: Is it raining outside?

And the decision we are deriving is:

Decision: Should we carry an umbrella?

The pseudo-code for this will look like as below:

```
IF (It is sunny outside) OR (It is raining outside)
THEN
    Carry an umbrella
ELSE
    Do not carry an umbrella
END
```

The different possible combinations for the above example are shown in Table 4.3.

Table 4.3 Different possibilities

Condition 1	Condition 2	Decision
Is it sunny outside?	Is it raining outside?	Should carry an umbrella?
Yes	Yes	Yes
Yes	No	Yes
No	Yes	Yes
No	No	No

4.4.3 NOT Operator

We use the 'NOT' operator to reverse a condition. When the condition is true, NOT will return false and vice versa. In some programming languages, the NOT operator is denoted by the "!" symbol.

The logical 'not' operator returns True if an expression is True; otherwise, it returns False.

For example, you can go to play if it is not raining; otherwise, you must stay indoors. Unlike the previous examples, here we have only one condition.

Condition: Is it raining?

Decision: Go out to play?

The pseudo-code for this will look like below:

```
IF NOT (It is raining)
THEN
    Go out to play
ELSE
    Stay indoors
END
```

Factz Funda

Scratch is a free programming language and is one of the most popular choices for teaching block-based coding to learners.

The possibilities in respect of the above pseudo-code are depicted in Table 4.4.

Table 4.4 Different possibilities

Is it raining?	Go out to play?
Yes	No
No	Yes

Factz Funda

'If' statement is one of the powerful conditional statements. 'If' statement is responsible for modifying the flow of execution of a program.

4.5 COMBINING LOGICAL OPERATORS

Sometimes, we need to combine different logical operators to create a complex expression.

With the help of the following activity, it can be understood well.

Activity 4.2

- Participate in the individual activity on **"Creating pseudo-code and flowchart based on combining logical operators."**
- Suppose *Kanika Gym* of your city is open on Monday between 9 AM to 12 PM OR on Thursday between 2 PM to 6 PM.
- Create a pseudo-code and flowchart for this situation.

```
IF (Day == Monday AND (Time >= 9 AM AND
Time <=12 PM)) OR
    (Day == Thursday AND (Time >= 2 PM
    AND Time <= 6 PM))
THEN
     Gym Open
ELSE
     Gym Closed
END
```

The corresponding flowchart for the above pseudo-code will be like below:

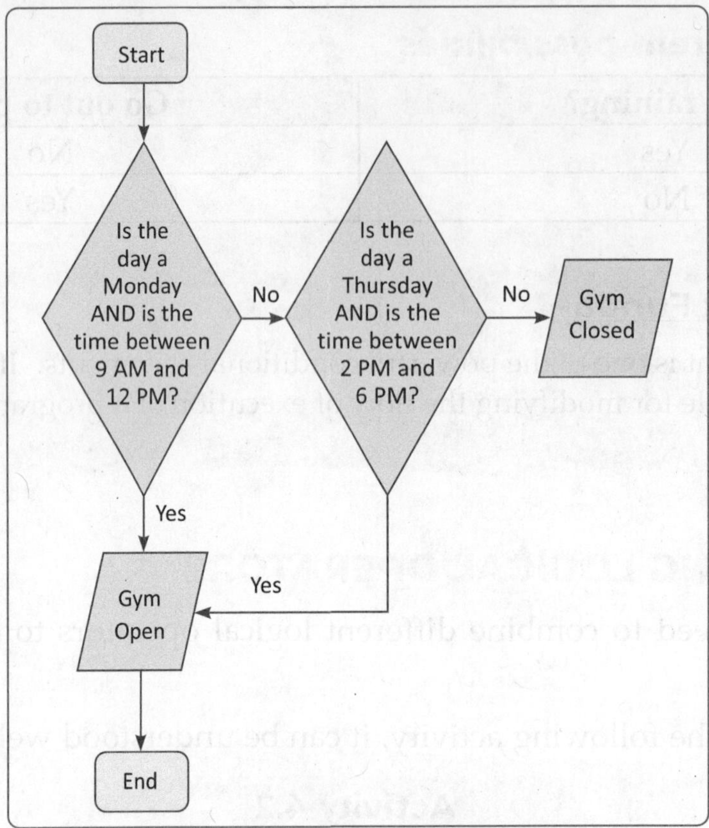

Figure 4.5 Flowchart

1. Consider the following pseudocode to answer the questions mentioned below;

```
IF (Day == Tuesday AND (Time >= 10 AM AND
Time <=2 PM)) OR
    (Day == Friday AND (Time >= 2 PM
    AND Time <= 5 PM))
THEN
    Library Open
ELSE
    Library Closed
END
```

1. Situation: Today is Tuesday, and the time is 2 PM. Is the library open now?

   (a) Yes (b) No

2. Situation: Today is Monday and the time is 10.30 AM. Is the library open now?

   (a) Yes (b) No

3. Situation: Today is Friday, and the time is 2.30 PM. Is the library open now?

   (a) Yes (b) No

4. Situation: Today is Wednesday, and the time is 10.30 AM. Is the library open now?

   (a) Yes (b) No

5. Situation: Today is Friday and the time is 4.30 PM. Is the library open now?

   (a) Yes (b) No

6. Situation: Today is Tuesday and the time is 3.30 PM. Is the library open now?

   (a) Yes (b) No

ANSWERS
1. (a) 2. (b) 3. (a) 4. (a) 5. (b) 6. (b)

Factz Funda

If-else statement is also called branching because a program decides which statement to execute based on the result of the evaluated condition.

4.6 RELATIONAL OPERATORS

In our previous example, we were introduced to some relational operators like greater than equals (>=), equals (==), and less than equals (<=).

The full list of relational operators is shown in Table 4.5.

Table 4.5 Relational operators

Operator	Symbol	Example	Meaning
Greater than	>	x > y	x greater than y
Equal to	==	x == y	x is equal to y
Less than	<	x < y	x is less than y
Greater than or equal to	>=	x >= y	x is either greater than or equal to y
Less than or equal to	<=	x <= y	x is either less than or equal to
Not equal to	!=	x! = y	x is not equal to y

Activity 4.3

- Participate in the individual activity on making a flowchart on **"Are you a teen?"**
- In this activity, you have to check if you are a child, teenager, or adult with the help of a flowchart created by you.
- Steps to create the flowchart:
  - Input your age
  - If age < 12, Then Child
  - Else If age > 12 and <=19, Then Teenager,
  - Else, If age > 19, Then adult
  - Print "child or teenager or adult" depending on the condition satisfied

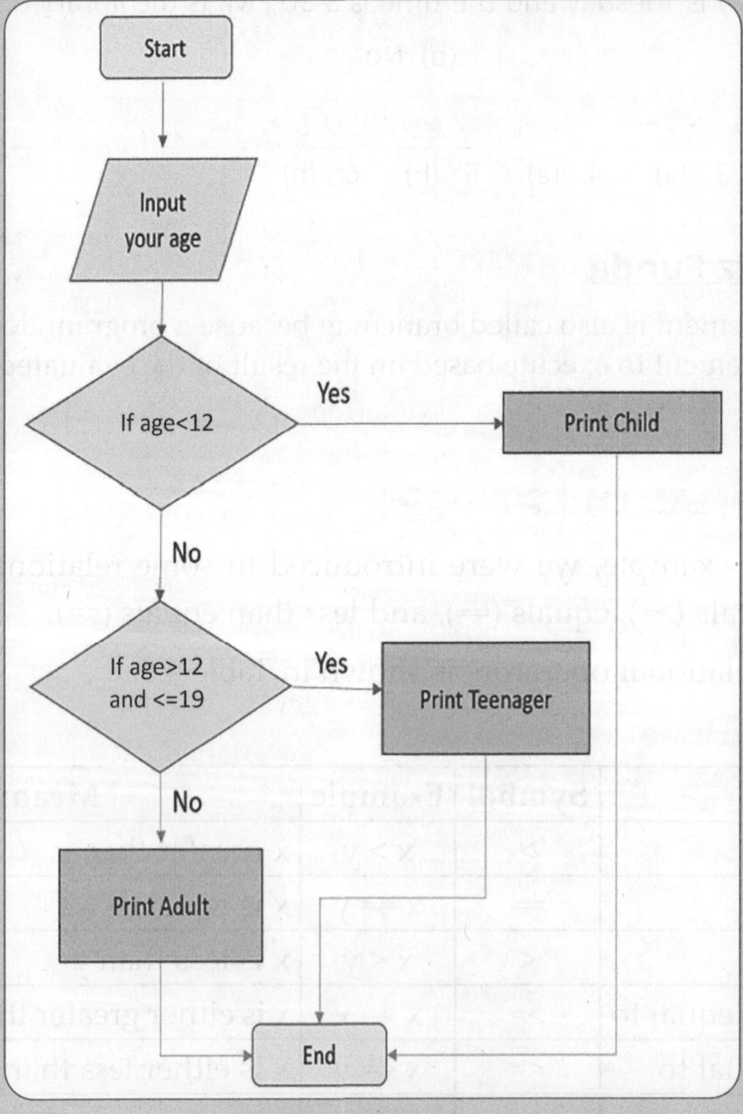

Figure 4.6 Flowchart "Are you a teen?"

Based on the flowchart 'Are you a teen?' (Figure 4.6), answer the questions given below:

1. The age of Ambika is 37 years. In which category will she fall?
   (a) Child (b) Teenager (c) Adult (d) None of the above
2. If Zahira is your friend and her age is 17 years. In which category will she fall?
   (a) Child (b) Teenager (c) Adult (d) None of the above
3. Basu Chatterjee's age is 11 years. In which category will he fall?
   (a) Child (b) Teenager (c) Adult (d) None of the above
4. If the age of Benson George is 15 years, then in which category will he fall?
   (a) Child (b) Teenager (c) Adult (d) None of the above

ANSWERS
1. (c) 2. (b) 3. (a) 4. (b)

4.7 NESTED CONDITIONAL STATEMENTS

We may have an 'if' and/ 'if else' statement inside another 'if' and/ 'if else' statement. This situation is called nesting in computer programming. Any number of these statements may be nested inside one another. Indentation is the only way to figure out the level of nesting. This may get confusing, so it must be avoided if it can be.

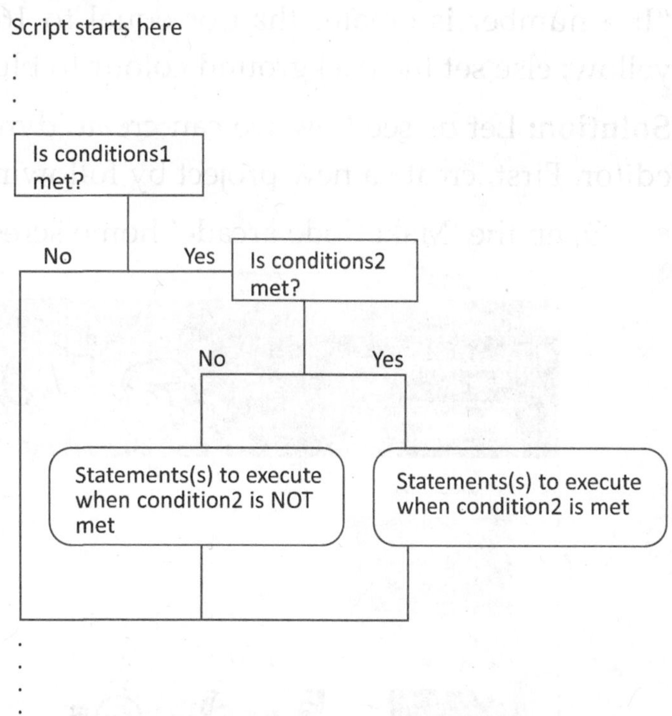

Figure 4.7: Nested conditional statement

Under certain circumstances, we might have to deal with complex scenarios where using a single if-else loop might not be enough. Suppose you want to check if a number is divisible by 2 or 3 or both 2 and 3. In this case, we first need an 'IF' condition to check if the number is divisible by 2. Within that condition, we can implement another 'IF' condition to check if the number is divisible by 3 or not. By doing so, we can check the divisibility of the number.

Project Time

Project 4.1

Aim: To create a dynamic background by using conditional statements in block coding.

Learning Outcomes:

- To learn how to use conditional statements in block coding.
- To learn how to use variables.
- To learn how to use logical operators.

Problem Statement: Creating dynamic backgrounds using in MakeCode editor is easy by using conditional statements. Find if a number is less than or greater than 16 and then change the background color in the MakeCode editor. These are the steps that need to be followed:

"If a number is greater than or equal to 16, then set the background colour to yellow; else set the background colour to blue."

Solution: Let us see how we can create dynamic backgrounds in the MakeCode editor. First, create a new project by following the steps given below:

- Open the 'MakeCode arcade' home screen.

Figure 4.8

- Click on the new project and name it "Dynamic background."

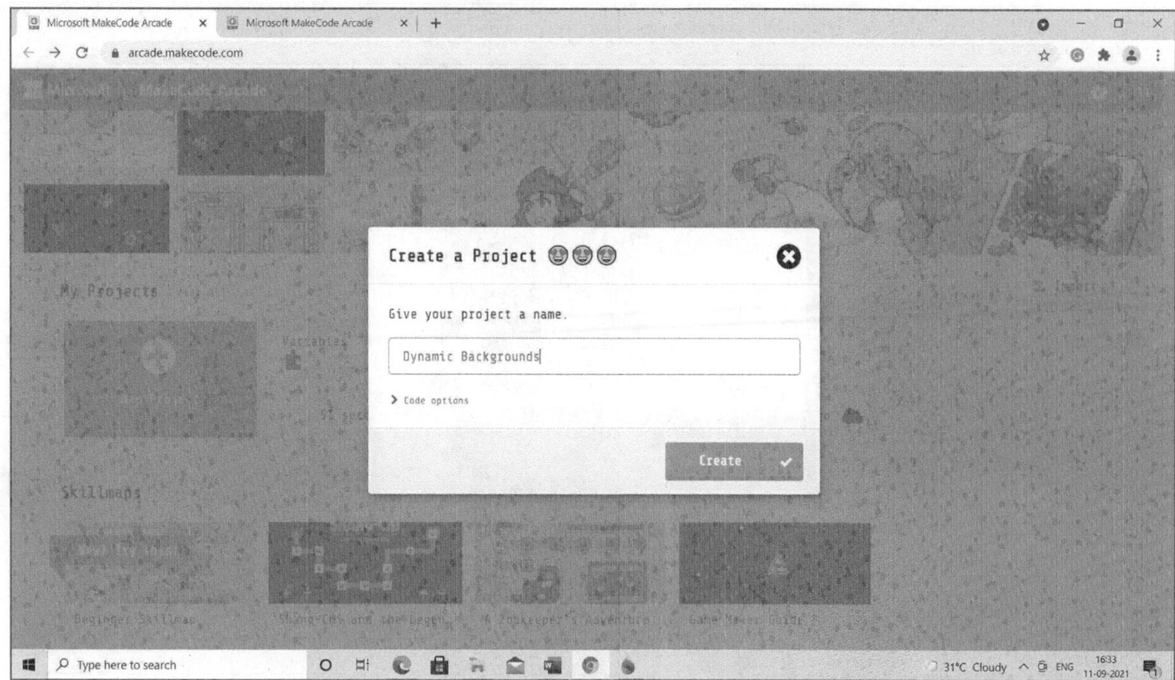

Figure 4.9

- Follow the following steps to complete the project:
- Step 1: Click on the variable menu on the left pane. Click on "Make a variable" and create a variable called "Height."

Figure 4.10

Step 2: Set height to 16. Choose an if-else block from the "Logic" section.

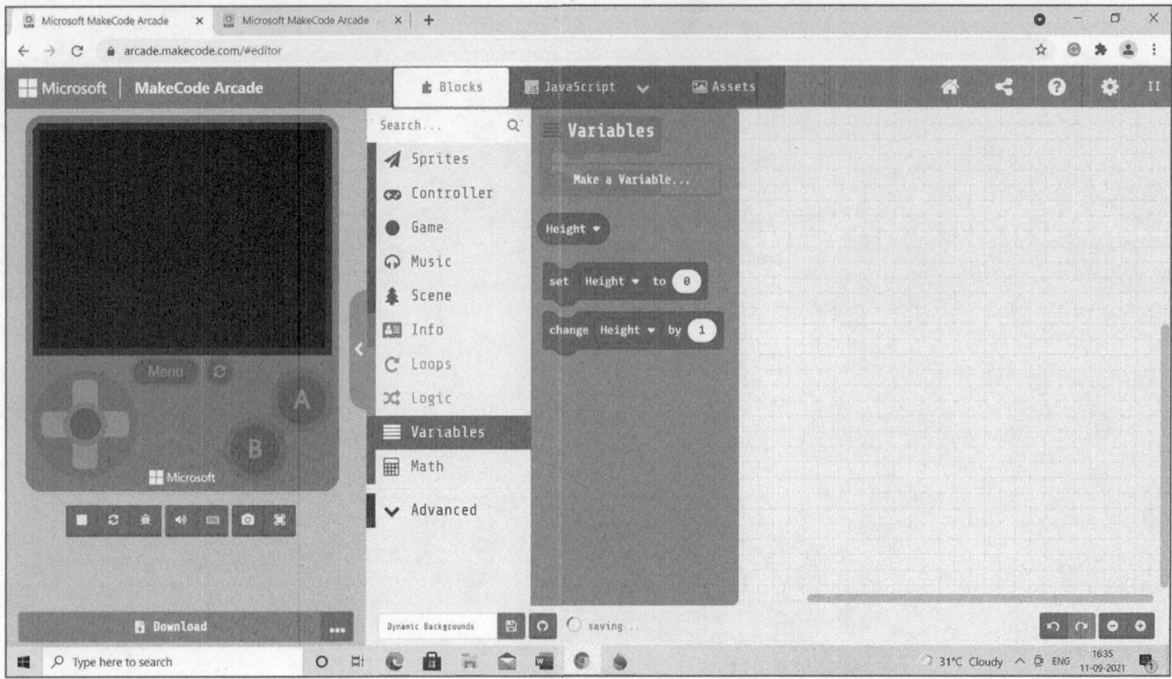

Figure 4.11

Step 3: Choose a Boolean 'AND' operator from the logic section and add it to the if-else block as shown here. Moreover, add two comparison operators to both the sides of the 'AND' condition.

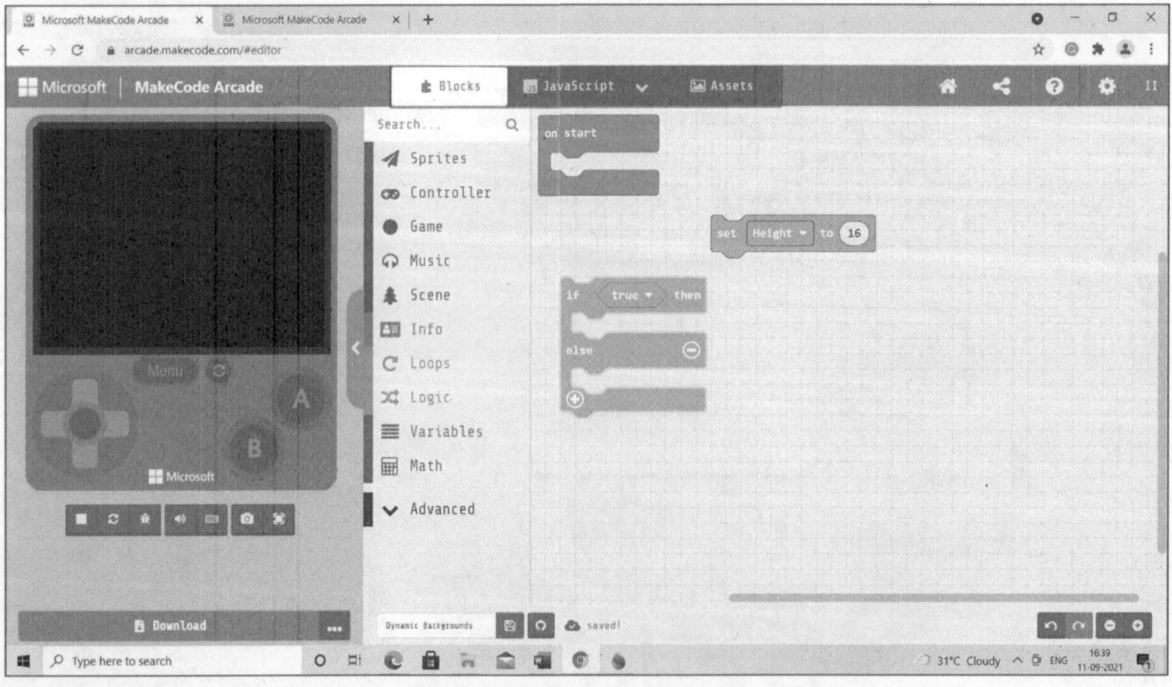

Figure 4.12

Step 4: Add the set background block from the "Scene" section to both if and else conditions. Choose different background conditions for the if and else blocks.

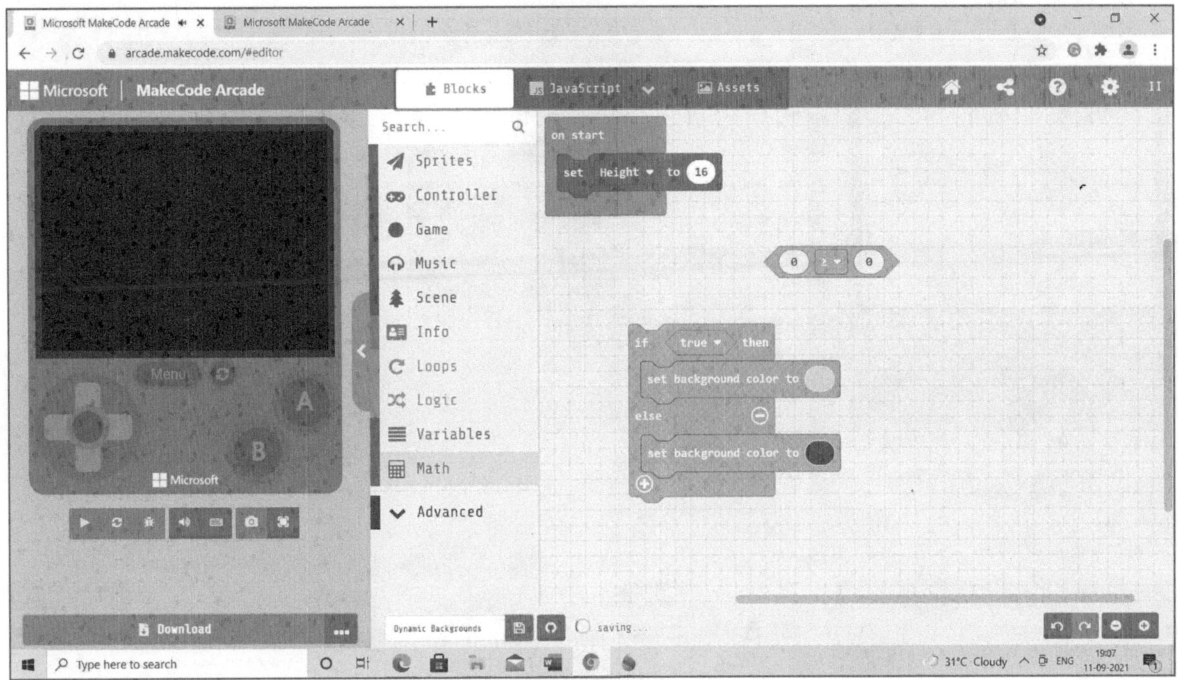

Figure 4.13

Step 5: Add two comparison operators to both sides of the AND condition.

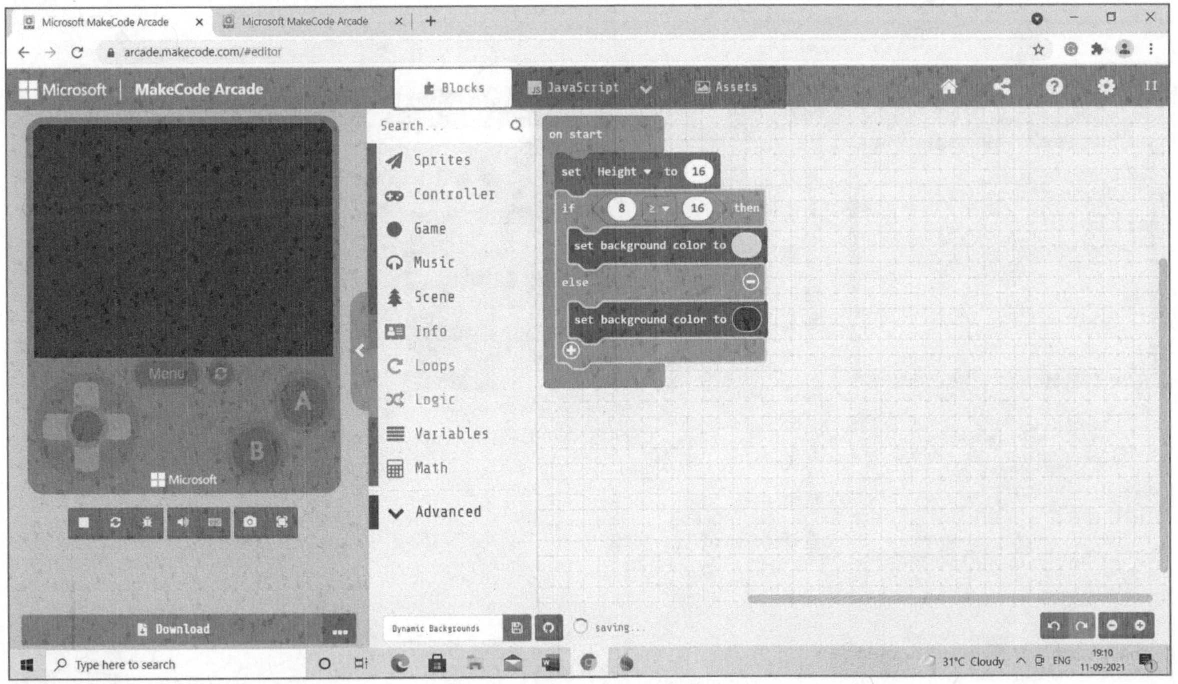

Figure 4.14

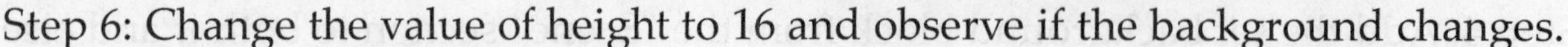
Step 6: Change the value of height to 16 and observe if the background changes.

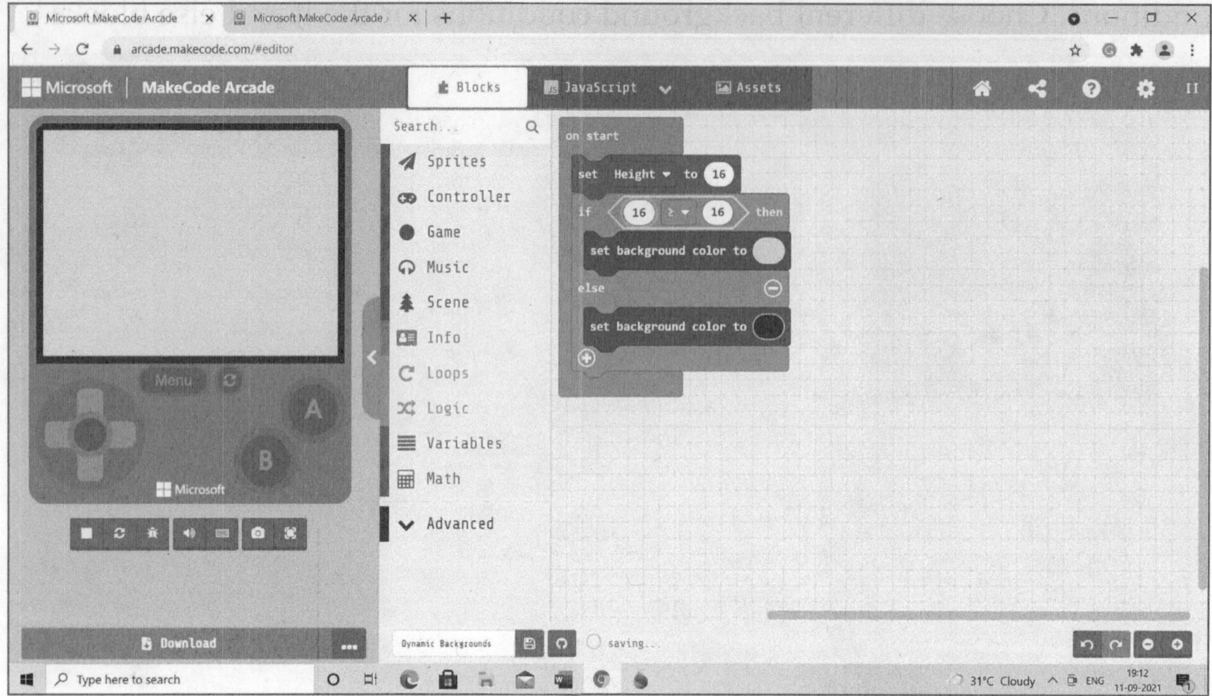

Figure 4.15

Step 7: Change the value of height to 18 and observe to which colour the background change.

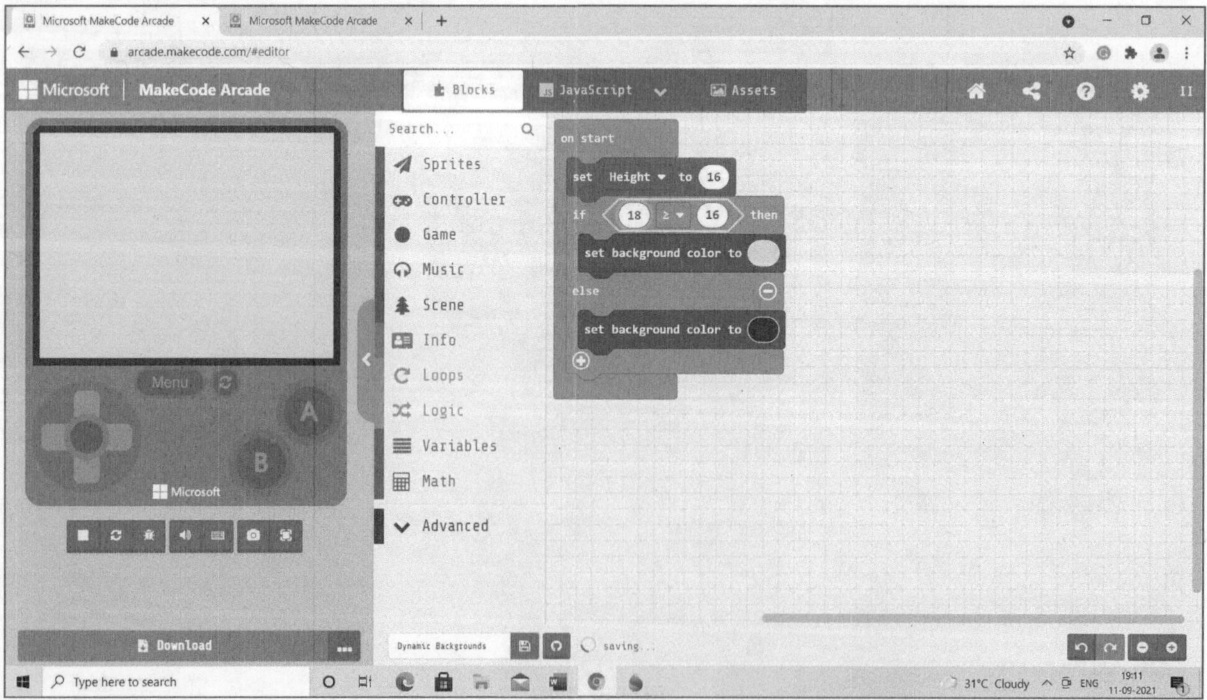

Figure 4.16

Step 8: Change the value of height to 7 and observe to which colour the background change.

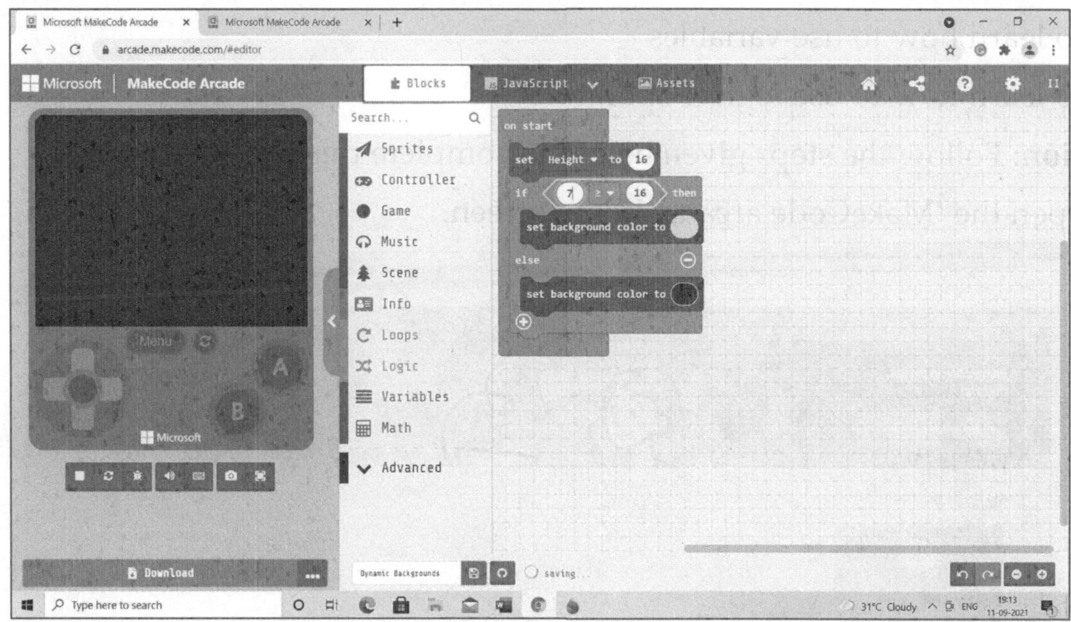

Figure 4.17

When you change the height to 8, the loop will go inside the if condition as the height is less than 16, the background colour will change to blue. But when we change the height to 18 or 16, it will complete the condition (greater than or equal to 16), the background colour becomes yellow.

What have we learned from this project?

We have learned how to create conditional statements.

What do you think will the output of the code be if you change the height to 15? That is correct! The background colour changes to green as the height is greater than 5 AND less than 20.

Project 4.2

Aim: To solve a remainder problem by using conditional statements in block coding.

Problem Statement: Using nested conditional statements, find if a number is divisible by 7 and 3 and then change the background colour in the MakeCode editor. These are the steps that need to be followed:

When a number is divisible by 7 and 3, then set the background colour to pink.

When a number is not divisible by both 7 and 3, then set the background colour to yellow.

Learning Outcome:

- To learn how to use nested conditional statements in block coding.
- To learn how to use variables
- To learn how to use logical operators

Solution: Follow the steps given below to complete this project:

- Open the 'MakeCode arcade' home screen.

Figure 4.18

- Click on the new project and name it "Dynamic background."

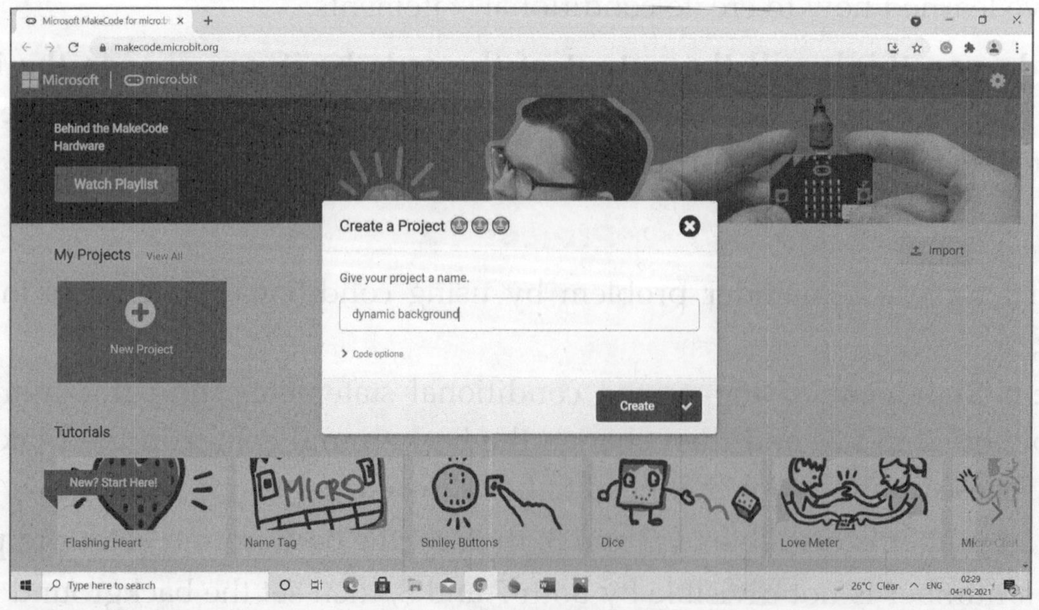

Figure 4.19

- Follow the following steps to complete the project:

Step 1: Click on the variable menu on the left pane. Click on "Make a variable" and create a variable called "Number."

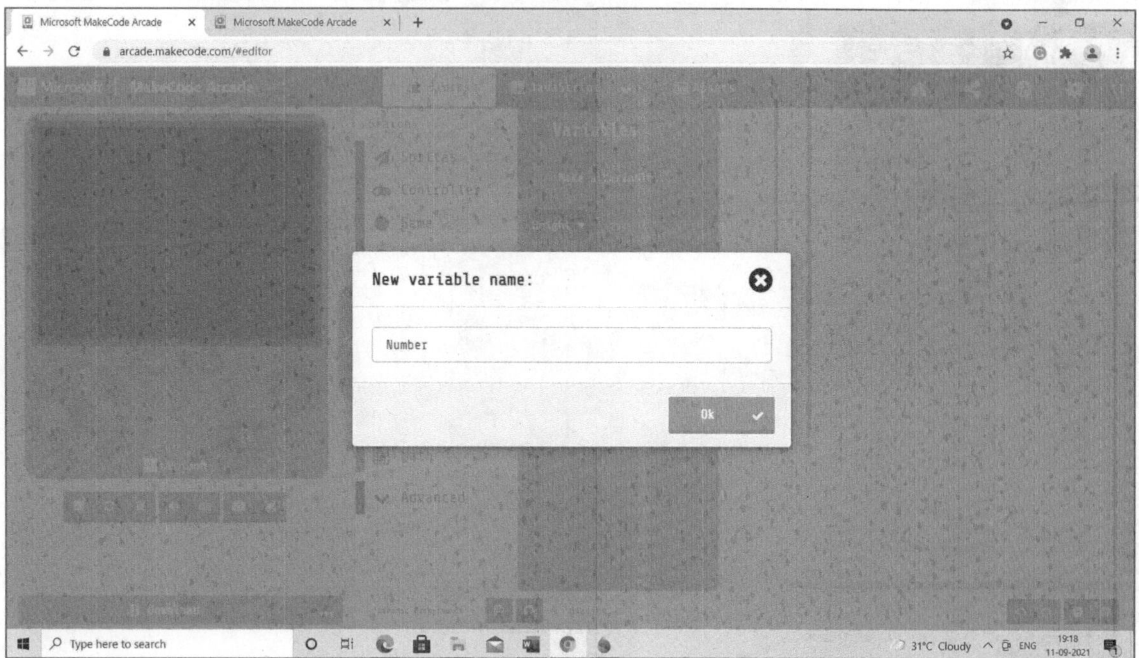

Figure 4.20

Step 2: Choose the Set block and set the value of the number to 15. Choose an if-else block from the "Logic" section.

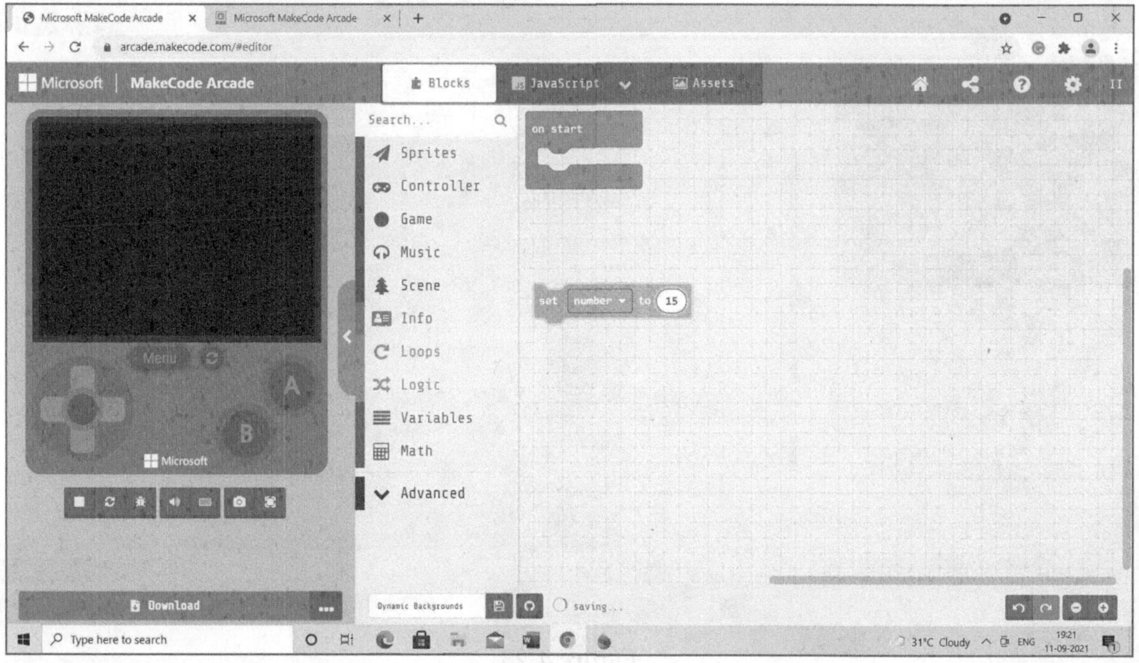

Figure 4.21

Step 3: Choose a comparison block from the logic section.

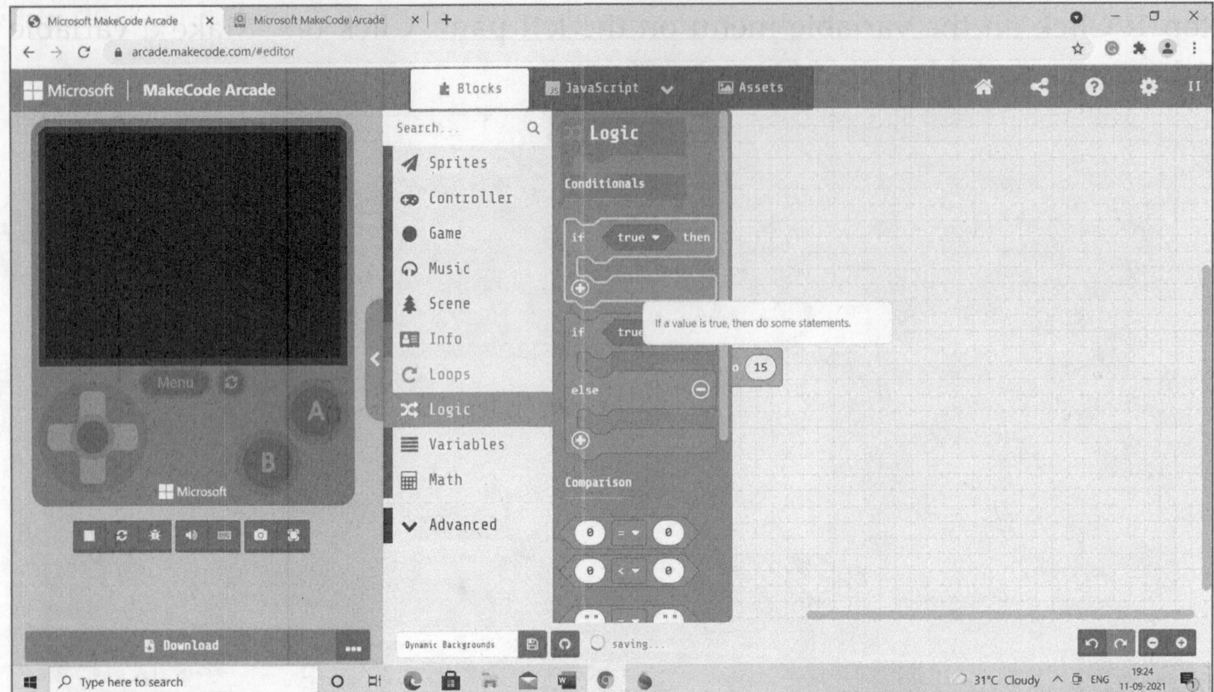

Figure 4.22

Step 4: Choose a remainder block from the "math" section and add it to the if block.

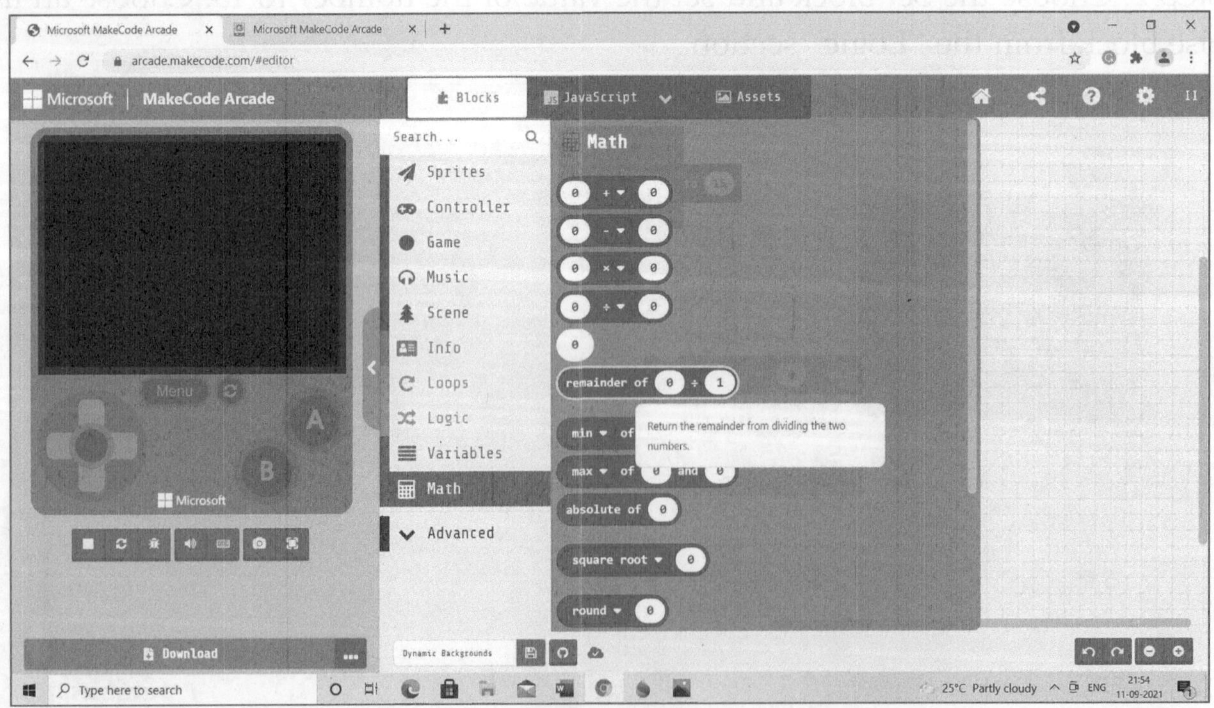

Figure 4.23

Step 5: Add a remainder block like step 4 and check if the number is the remainder on dividing by 7 is zero.

Step 6: Add the set background colours to both if and else blocks.

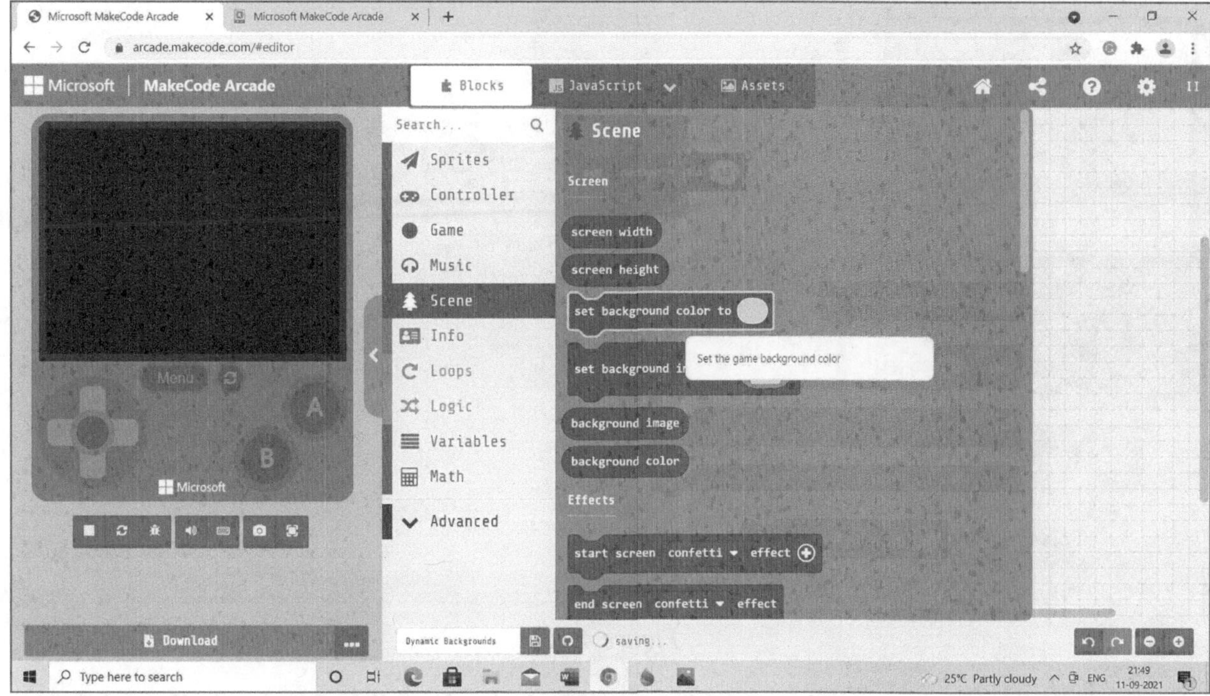

Figure 4.24

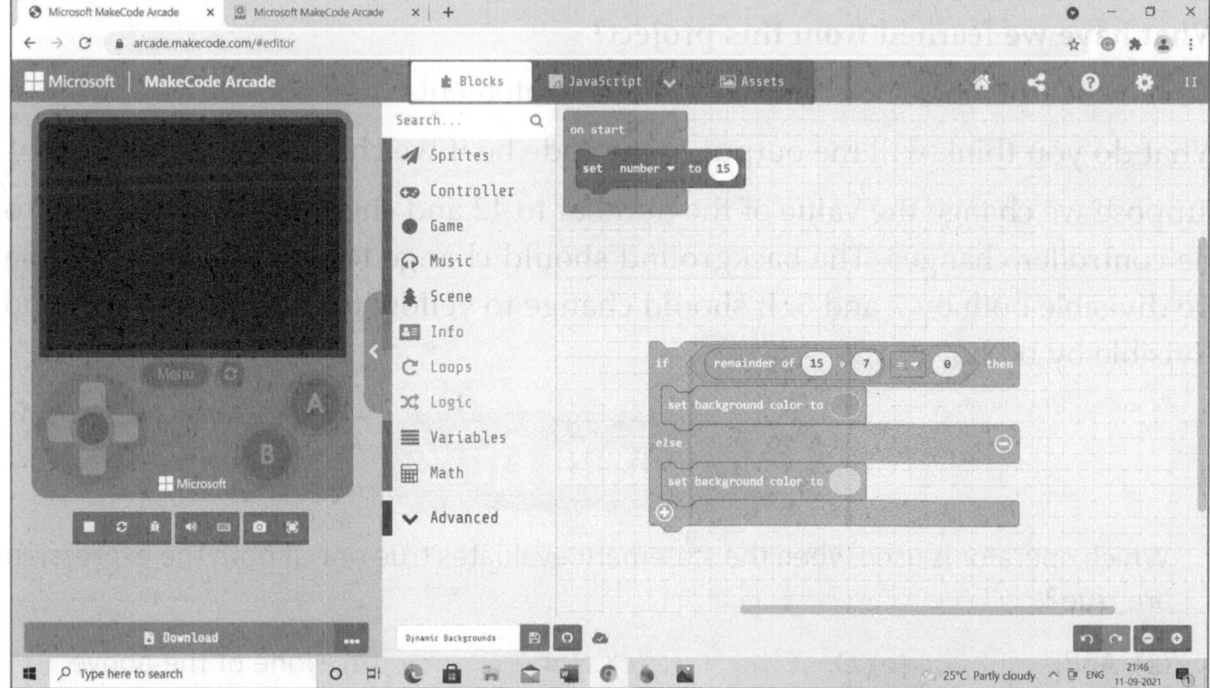

Figure 4.25

Background colour changes to pink when the input number is 21.

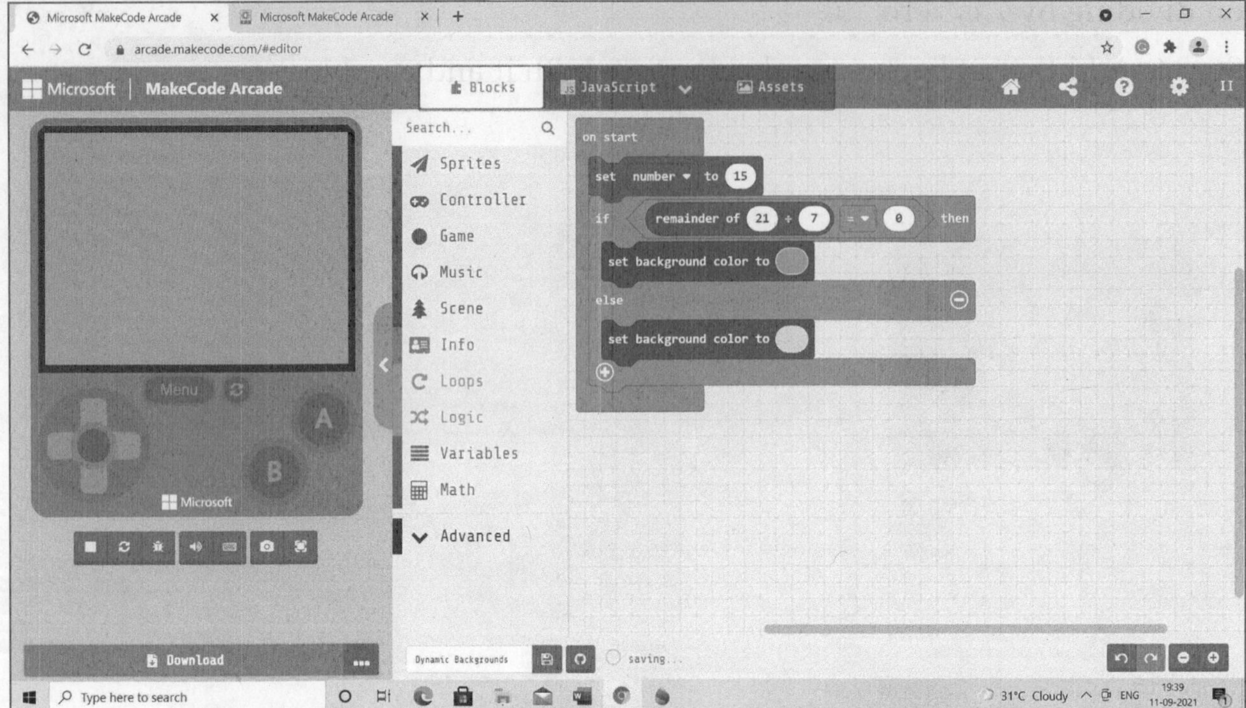

Figure 4.26

Result: When we change the number to 21, it is divisible by both 7 and 3, and hence, the background colour will change to pink.

What have we learned from this project?

We have learned how to create conditional statements.

What do you think will the output of the code be if we change the number to 44?

Suppose we change the value of the number to 42 and check if the background of the controller changes. The background should change to pink for numbers that are divisible both by 7 and 3. It should change to yellow for numbers that are not divisible by both 7 and 3.

1. Which operator is used when the statement evaluates true only if both the expressions are true?

   (a) And (b) Or (c) Not (d) None of the above

2. Which operator is used when the statement evaluates true only when only one of the expressions is true?

   (a) Not (b) And (c) Or (d) None of the above

3. Which operator is used to reverse a condition?

   (a) And (b) Not (c) Or (d) None of the above

ANSWERS
1. (a) 2. (c) 3. (b)

SUMMARY

- An operator is defined as a symbol that will perform mathematical operations on variables or on values.
- There are seven types of operators: Arithmetic Operators, Relational Operators, Assignment Operators, Logical Operators, Membership Operators, Identity Operators, and Bitwise Operators.
- Seven Arithmetic operators are used for different mathematical operations (Addition, Subtraction, Multiplication, Division, Exponentiation, Floor division, and Modulus)
- Relational Operators are also called comparison operators that are used to compare values.
- There are six relational operators: greater than, less than, equal to, not equal to, greater than or equal to, less than or equal to.
- Assignment operators perform an operation and assign a value.
- There are eight assignment operators:
- Logical Operators can combine conditions, and there are three logical operators: And, Or, Not.
- Conditional statements execute in a sequence when there is no condition around the statements.
- Membership operators check if a value is in another value or not. There are two membership operators: in and not in.
- Identity operators check whether two values are identical or not.
- Bitwise operators operate on values bit by bit, and there are six bitwise operators.
- The logic in coding terms is called conditions.
- Logical operators perform like Boolean variables and return either TRUE or FALSE.
- Conditional Statements programming is used to make decisions based on the conditions.
- AND operator is used to determining if two or more conditions are true.

- When all the conditions are true, the AND operator returns TRUE. When any one of the conditions fail, the AND operator returns FALSE.
- The OR operator is used to determine if either one of two or more conditions is TRUE.
- The 'NOT' operator is used to reverse or negate a condition.
- The logical not operator returns True when an expression is True; otherwise, it returns False.
- 'If' statement is responsible for modifying the flow of execution of a program.
- 'If' statement is always used with a condition.
- The condition in the 'if' statement is evaluated first before executing any statement inside the body of 'If.'
- If-else statement is also called branching because a program decides which statement to execute based on the result of the evaluated condition.
- When we have an 'if, and/ if else' statement inside another 'if' and/ 'if else' statement, then this situation is called nesting in computer programming.

PRACTICE TIME

(A) True/False Type Questions

1. Logical operators may be used to make decisions in our code.
2. There are eight types of operators.
3. Seven Arithmetic operators are used for different mathematical operations.
4. There are six relational operators.
5. Assignment operators perform an operation and assign a value.
6. Logical Operators can combine conditions, and there are five logical operators.
7. Conditional statements execute in a sequence when there is no condition around the statements.
8. The logical Not' operator returns True if an expression is True; otherwise, it returns False.
9. 'If' statement is always used with a condition.
10. Conditional Statements programming is used to make decisions based on the conditions.

ANSWERS							
1. T	2. F (seven)	3. T	4. T	5. T	6. F (3)	7. T	8. T
9. T	10. T						

(B) Fill in the blanks

1. An ____________ is a symbol that will perform mathematical operations on variables or on values.
2. ____________ Operators check whether two values are identical.
3. ____________ Operators are also called comparison operators that are used to compare values.
4. The ____________ operator is used to determine if either one of two or more conditions is TRUE.
5. ____________ operator is used to determining when two or more conditions are true.
6. There are ____________ assignment operators.
7. ____________ operators perform like Boolean variables and return either TRUE or FALSE.
8. Membership operators check whether a value is in another value or not. There are ____________ membership operators.
9. ____________ statement is responsible for modifying the flow of execution of a program.
10. When we have an 'if, and/ if else' statement inside another 'if' and/ 'if else' statement, then this situation is called ____________ in computer programming.

ANSWERS					
1. operator	2. Identity	3. Relational	4. OR	5. AND	6. Eight
7. Logical	8. two	9. 'If'	10. Nesting		

(C) Very Short Answers Questions

1. What are operators?
2. What do you mean by Nestling?
3. Which operators are known as comparison operators too?
4. How many logical operators are there?
5. Name all the logical operators.

(D) Short Answer Questions

1. Explain different types of logical operators with examples.
2. Explain with an example how to combine different logical operators.

3. Write the pseudo-code using logical operators to decide if today is Ananya Coffee-shop open or closed. Monday-Friday: open; Sunday: Closed; 1st and 3rd Saturday: Closed; 2nd and 4th Saturday: open)
4. Mention the names of all relational operators.

(E) High Order Thinking Skill Questions (HOTS)

1. Why are logical operators used in coding?
2. Based on the given below pseudo-code, answer the following questions (Question i-iv):

```
IF (Day == Saturday OR Day == Sunday
IF (Time >= 12 AM AND Time <=12 PM))
THEN
        Shop closed
ELSE
        Shop open
ELSE
        Shop open
END
```

(i) Situation: Today is Monday, and the time is 10.30 AM. Is the shop open?

(a) True (b) False

(ii) Situation: Today is Friday, and the time is 1.30 AM. Is the shop closed?

(a) True (b) False

(iii) Situation: Today is Wednesday and the time is 4.30 AM. Is the shop open?

a) True b) False

(iv) Situation: Today is Saturday and the time is 8.30 PM. Is the shop closed?

(a) True b) False

(F) Projects

1. Create an if-else block with a NOT condition and set two different background colours in block coding.
2. Create an if-else block with an OR condition and set two different background images in block coding.

3. Create a nested if-else block to check if a number is divisible by 7 or 3 or both.
4. Create a nested if-else block using NOT to check if a number is a power of 2 or 3 or both.
5. Create a program using conditional statements for Meerut Sports Fest. If an event occurs, THEN what happens? Use the following guidelines:
   - If a player crosses the finish line first
   - If a referee blows the whistle
   - If a ball goes outside the boundary
   - If the time limit is reached
   - If a player touches a player during tag

5 Loops Using Block Coding

Structure

In this chapter, you will learn:

- What are loops?
- Different types of loops
- How to increment loops?
- Concept of nested loops

INTRODUCTION

A loop may be defined as a shape produced by a curve that bends around and crosses itself. Grammatically, loop means encircling. A loop may also be defined as a structure, series, or process, the end of which is connected to the beginning. We see various loops in our daily life. For example, the water cycle is one type of loop. When you are running along the borders of the ground of your school, it makes a loop if you return to the beginning point.

Loop is regarded as one of the basic logical structures of computer programming. The necessity for defining the loop in a computer program is clear due to various reasons that are based on the tasks to be performed. Computers perform particular tasks repeatedly when loops are used with the proper definition. Therefore, computer programming languages require loops for the execution of the codes as many times as required.

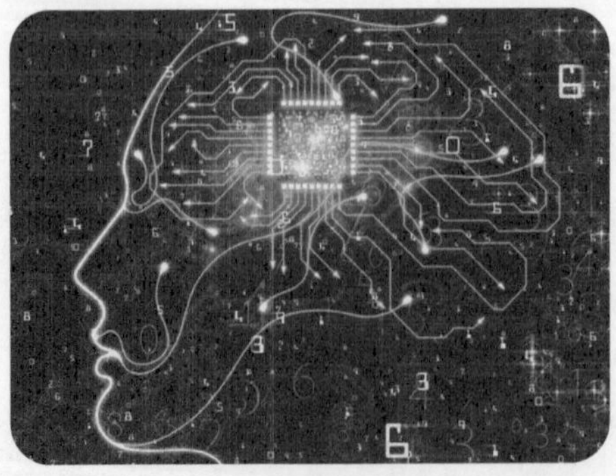

Figure 5.1

In this chapter, we shall study what loops are in programming/coding, how to increment loops, types of loops, and the concept of nested loops.

Learning Objectives:

At the end of this chapter, you will be able to:

- Have an idea of what loops are and how they are used in programming.
- Incrementing loops.
- Know different types of loops.
- Know entry and exit criteria in loops and their usage.
- Break and continue statements.
- Understand the concept of nested loops.

5.1 LOOPS

For understanding the loop, consider the case of your coming to school. What are the different steps for going to school and coming back home? Think and write.

Perhaps the steps might be as follows:

- Walk out of the home to the bus stop
- Wait for the school bus
- Get on the school bus
- Arrive at school
- Walk to the school and then to the classroom
- Attending the school/participating in all activities
- Walk to the school gate
- Get on the school bus.
- Get down at the bus stop near your home
- Walk to your home from the bus stop.

Thus, your walk to school is a loop you perform every day. Similarly, there are many more tasks in our day-to-day life that we repeat at specific intervals, like eating meals, taking a bath, going to the weekly market, etc. These are few examples of loops.

Figure 5.2

Activity 5.1

- Participate in the class discussion on **"Examples of Loops in Our Lives."**
- All the students will participate in the discussion on the topic that will be initiated by the teacher in the class.
- One student will record all the examples shared by the participants and will share the complete list with the whole class.

There is a very similar concept to this in programming, where we need to repeat certain lines of code at a specific interval or till a specified condition is met.

In programming, repetition of a line or a block of code is also known as iteration. A loop is an algorithm that executes a block of code multiple times till the time a specified condition is met. Therefore, we can say that a loop iterates a block of code multiple times till the time mentioned condition is satisfied.

Figure 5.3

In coding, loops allow us to repeat something again and again. Loops will repeat until we give instructions for the computer to stop. In some cases, we might tell our computer to stop after it has repeated the loop a certain number of times. In other cases, we may tell our computer to stop once a certain condition is met.

Factz Funda

An iterator is defined as an object that allows a programmer to traverse through all the elements of a collection, regardless of its specific implementation.

For example, consider that you want to print alphabets A to C on the screen. We can do so by printing the values A, B and C by writing three lines of code.

Let us now look at the following pseudocode:

```
Start
This program demonstrates printing alphabets A to C
Print A
Print B
Print C
End
Output:
A
B
C
```

Figure 5.4

This was easy. Now, consider a requirement where we need to print numbers in incremental order from 1 to 4000. Although it is possible to print it following the above pseudocode, it will get a very tedious and lengthy process. This is where loops come into the picture to make this task easier. We can use the concept of loops and get the desired output by writing just a few lines of code.

Table 5.1 Some Examples of Loops:

- A song that is intentionally put on a repeat mode just to deep dive into the feeling.
- Salary preparation software is used by some organizations.
- Software used to get the printout of salary slips of all employees of an organization.
- Water Cycle

5.2 INCREMENTING LOOPS

Loops provide the facility to execute a block of code repetitively, based on a condition. This block of code is executed repeatedly till the time a specified condition remains true. This condition is checked based on the loop's control variable. Whenever this condition results in false, the loop terminates.

It is very important to keep this thing in mind while programming that the condition should result false at a certain point in time. Otherwise, this block of code will enter an infinite loop.

Execution of loops is based on iterations. To run a block of code in a loop, one needs to set a condition and set its number of iterations. Each time the condition is true, and the block of code executes once; it is counted to be one iteration. Before moving to the next iteration, one needs to increase the count of iteration to two. This is called incrementing a loop.

Factz Funda

We use the range () function to loop through a set of code a specified number of times. The range () function returns a sequence of numbers, starting from 0 (zero) by default, and increments by 1 (one), and ends at a specified number.

For example, if we need to print numbers 0 to 4, we will execute a block of code with a Print statement in five iterations. With each passing iteration, we will increment the count by one.

The two important benefits of loops are given below:

- Reduces lines of code
- Code becomes easier to understand

Let us understand loops with the help of a flowchart. The flowchart given in Figure 5.5 prints the numbers 1 to 9.

Here, every time the condition (Count < 9) is true, "Print count" gets executed. So, we do not have to write the "Print" statement multiple times. The loop takes care of that. The important point to note is that every loop must have an exit condition. In this example, the exit condition is (Count < 9). The loop will exit when the condition becomes false.

Also, most loops will have a variable which in programming terms is called a counter variable. The counter variable keeps record of how many times the loop is executed. In this

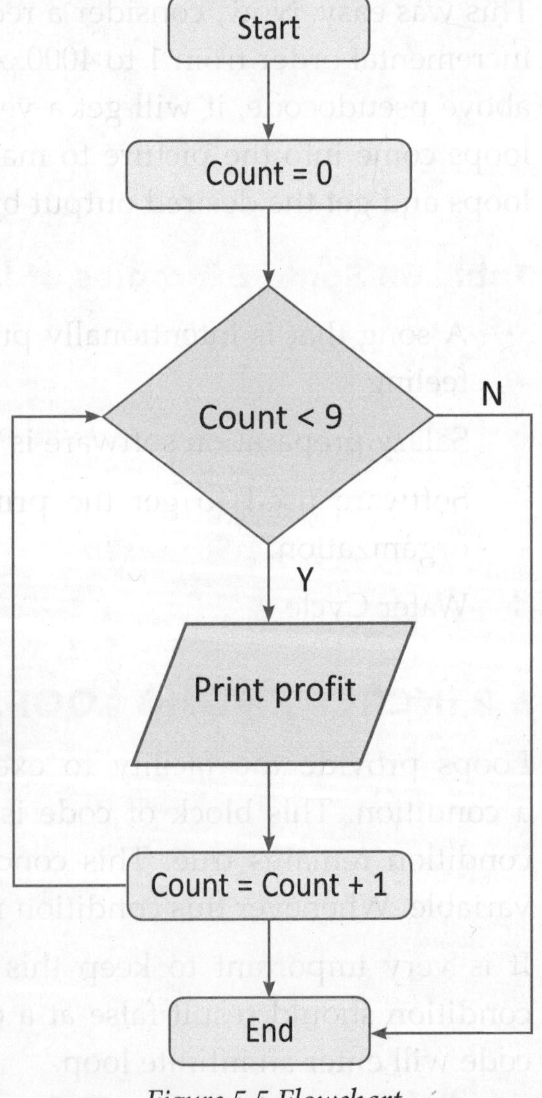

Figure 5.5 Flowchart

example, the "count" variable is our counter. Often, counter variables are incremented within the loop.

Factz Funda

A loop statement allows users to execute a statement or group of statements multiple times.

5.3 DIFFERENT TYPES OF LOOPS

Loops make our code more manageable, efficient, and organized. The different types of loops are as follows:

- While Loop
- For Loop
- Nested Loop

Figure 5.6

5.3.1 The While Loop:

'While' Loops are also called 'conditional' loops. The 'While' loop can execute a set of commands till the condition is true. Once the condition is met, then the loop is finished.

Thus, 'while' loops are those loops that will continue to go until a condition is no longer true. What is the reason they are called 'while' loops? This is due to the fact that the code will repeat while a condition is still true. We can think of while loops as telling our app "while this happens, repeat this" or "while this hasn't changed, repeat this."

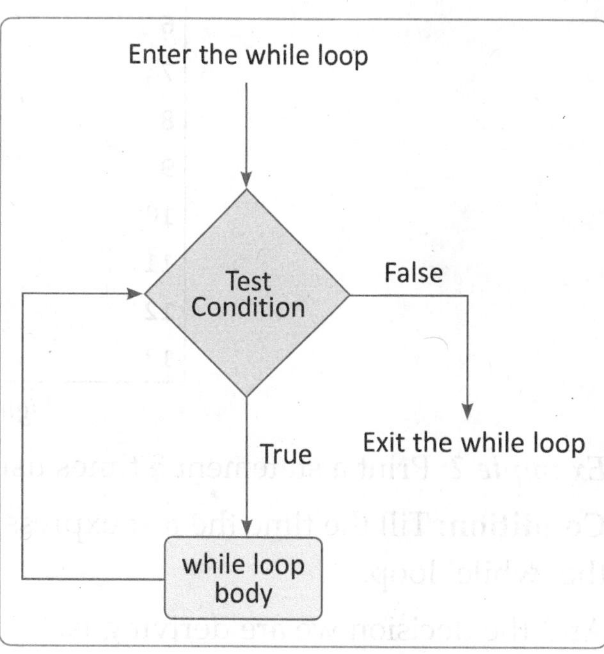

Figure 5.7

Consider the following examples:

Example 1: Print number from 1 to 13.

Here, if we want to derive the loop from this scenario, we have the following conditions:

Condition: Write from 1 to 13.

And the decision we are deriving is:

Decision: Have we reached 13?

Based on this, we can write the pseudocode as below:

```
y=0
While y < 13
      y+=1
      Print(y)
```

Figure 5.8

This is the output/result for the code:

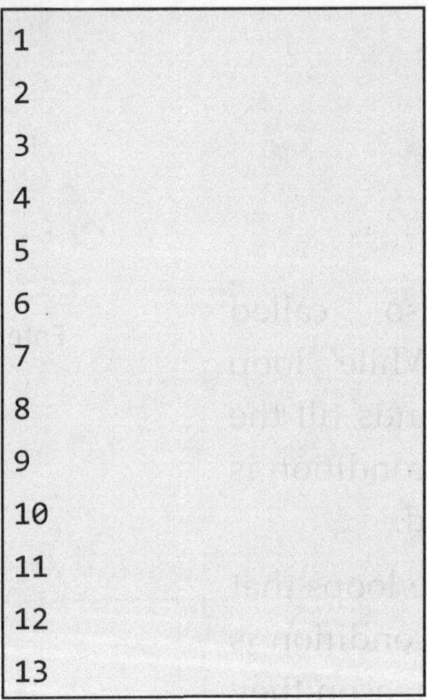

```
1
2
3
4
5
6
7
8
9
10
11
12
13
```

Figure 5.9

Example 2: Print a statement 5 times using a while loop.

Condition: Till the time the test expression remains true, we will run the body of the 'while' loop.

And the decision we are deriving is:

Decision: Have we printed the statement 5 times?

Based on this, we may write the pseudocode as below:

```
y=0
while y < 5
      y+=1
      Print("I will exercise for 30 minutes daily.")
```

Figure 5.10

This is the output/result for the code:

```
I will exercise for 30 minutes daily.
I will exercise for 30 minutes daily.
I will exercise for 30 minutes daily.
I will exercise for 30 minutes daily.
I will exercise for 30 minutes daily.
```

Figure 5.11

Example 3: Print a statement 4 times. After that, print a different statement.

Condition: Till the time the test expression remains true, we will run the body of while loop printing statement 1, and after the condition is false, we will print statement 2.

And the decision we are deriving is:

Decision: Have we printed the statement 1 four times, if yes then print statement 2.

Based on this, we can write the below pseudocode:

```
y=0
while y < 4
        y+=1
          print ("I am a hardworking and sincere guy.")
else
          print ("Welcome, Sir!")
```

Figure 5.12

This is the output/result for the code:

```
I am a hardworking and sincere guy.
I am a hardworking and sincere guy.
I am a hardworking and sincere guy.
I am a hardworking and sincere guy.
Welcome, Sir!
```

Figure 5.13

Example 4: Print number from 12 to 1

Condition: Till the time the test expression remains true, we will run the body of the while loop printing statement, and after the condition is false, the loop will stop.

And the decision we are deriving is:

Decision: Have we printed 1?

Based on this we can write the below pseudocode:

```
x=12
while x==1
print(x)
x-=1
```

Figure 5.14

This is the result of the code

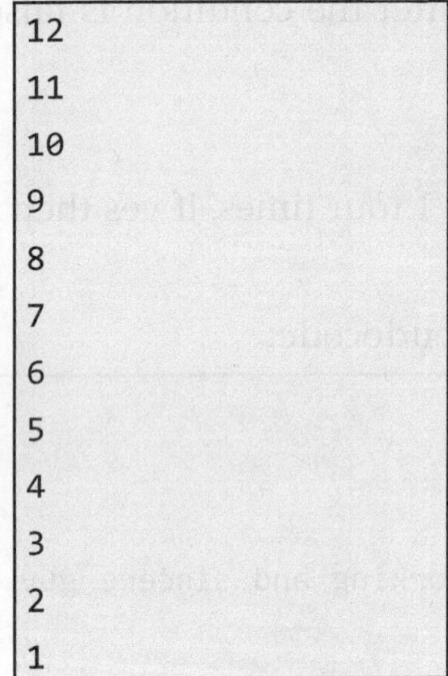

```
12
11
10
9
8
7
6
5
4
3
2
1
```

Figure 5.15

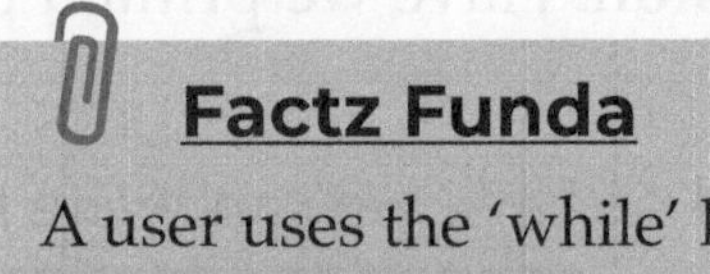

5.3.2 The 'For' Loop

'For' loop is needed for iterating over a sequence. A 'for' loop executes a specific number of times.

Thus, 'For' loops will repeat a block of code a set number of times as directed. The reason these loops are called 'for' loops is that we can tell our app how many times we want it to repeat the code. We can think about for loops as telling our app, "Repeat this, for 12 times" or "Repeat this, for five times."

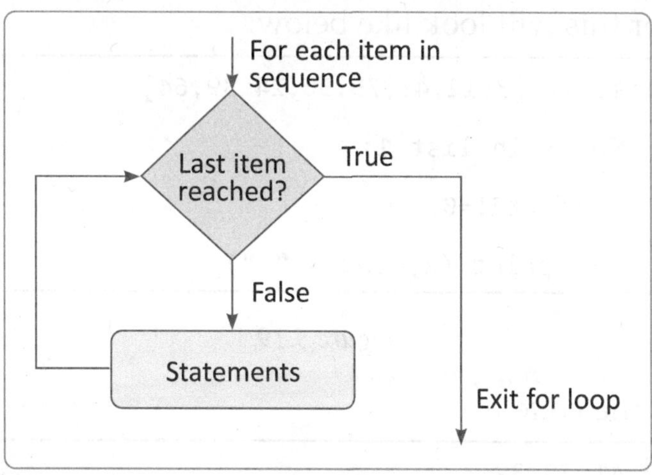

Figure 5.16

'For' loops use a variable to count how many times the code has been repeated, and it is called a 'counter.' We control how many times the loop repeats by setting where the counter starts and ends. We also set how much the counter goes up by each time the code repeats. In most cases, the counter increases by one each time the loop repeats.

Consider the following examples:

Example 1: We need to print a statement six times using the 'for' loop. The pseudo-code for this will look like below:

```
for i in range(6)
print("Brave persons never die.")
i++
```

Figure 5.17

Range (6) used in the above snippet returns a sequence of numbers from 0 to 5. This is the result for the code:

```
Brave persons never die.
Brave persons never die.
Brave persons never die.
Brave persons never die.
Brave persons never die.
Brave persons never die.
```

Figure 5.18

Example 2: Use 'for' loop to print all the odd numbers from a list.

The pseudo code for this will look like below:

```
list 1= [3,12,41,75.36,24,39,64]
  for x in list 1:
    if x%2!=0:
      print (x, end = " ")
```

Figure 5.19

This is the result of the code

```
3 41 75 39
```

Figure 5.20

Example 3: Use for loop to print all the even numbers from a list.
The pseudo-code for this will look like below:

```
list 1= [3,12,41,75.36,24,39,64]
  for x in list 1:
    if x%2!==0:
      print (x, end = " ")
```

Figure 5.21

This is the result for the code:

```
12 36 24 64
```

Figure 5.22

Factz Funda

A 'For' loop is to be used when the user is sure that exactly how many iterations have to be carried out. That can be the case while dealing with arrays, array lists, etc.

Figure 5.23

5.3.3 The Nested Loop

Any loop in the program may contain another loop inside it. When there is a loop inside another loop, it is called a nested loop. How it works is that the first success condition of the outer loop triggers the inner loop, which runs and reaches completion. This combination of loops inside a loop is helpful while working with requirements where the user wants to work on multiple conditions simultaneously. There is no restriction on how many loops can be nested inside a loop.

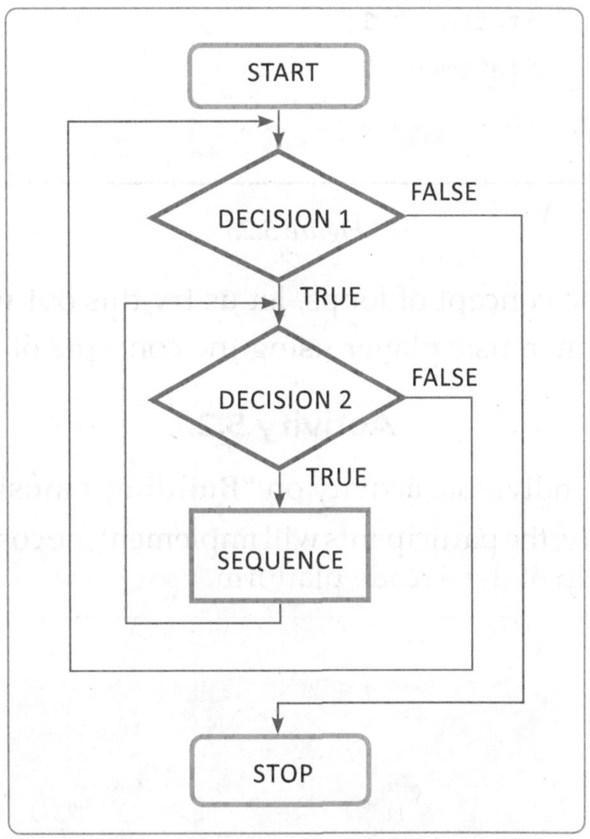

Figure 5.24

To understand the concept of Nested loops better, consider an example of an Analogue clock. An analogue clock has one hand as the nested loop, and every full rotation knocks the minute hand on by one and so on. We can take this even further to say that clocks are just a form of the counting system. This is how nested loops work in real life.

Factz Funda

When the user is not careful with the implementation of loops, then it may become an infinite loop. In an infinite loop, the program will execute a block of code forever until the computer runs out of CPU memory.

An example of a nested loop is given below:

```
While (loop-condition)
{
  While (loop-condition)
  {
     Statement 1;
     Statement 2;
  }
}
```

Figure 5.25

Now that we know the concept of loops, let us try this out with block coding. We will build a very simple music player using the concepts of loops.

Activity 5.2

- Participate in the individual activity on **"Building a music player."**
- During this activity, the participants will implement the concept of incrementing loops with the help of the Arcade platform.

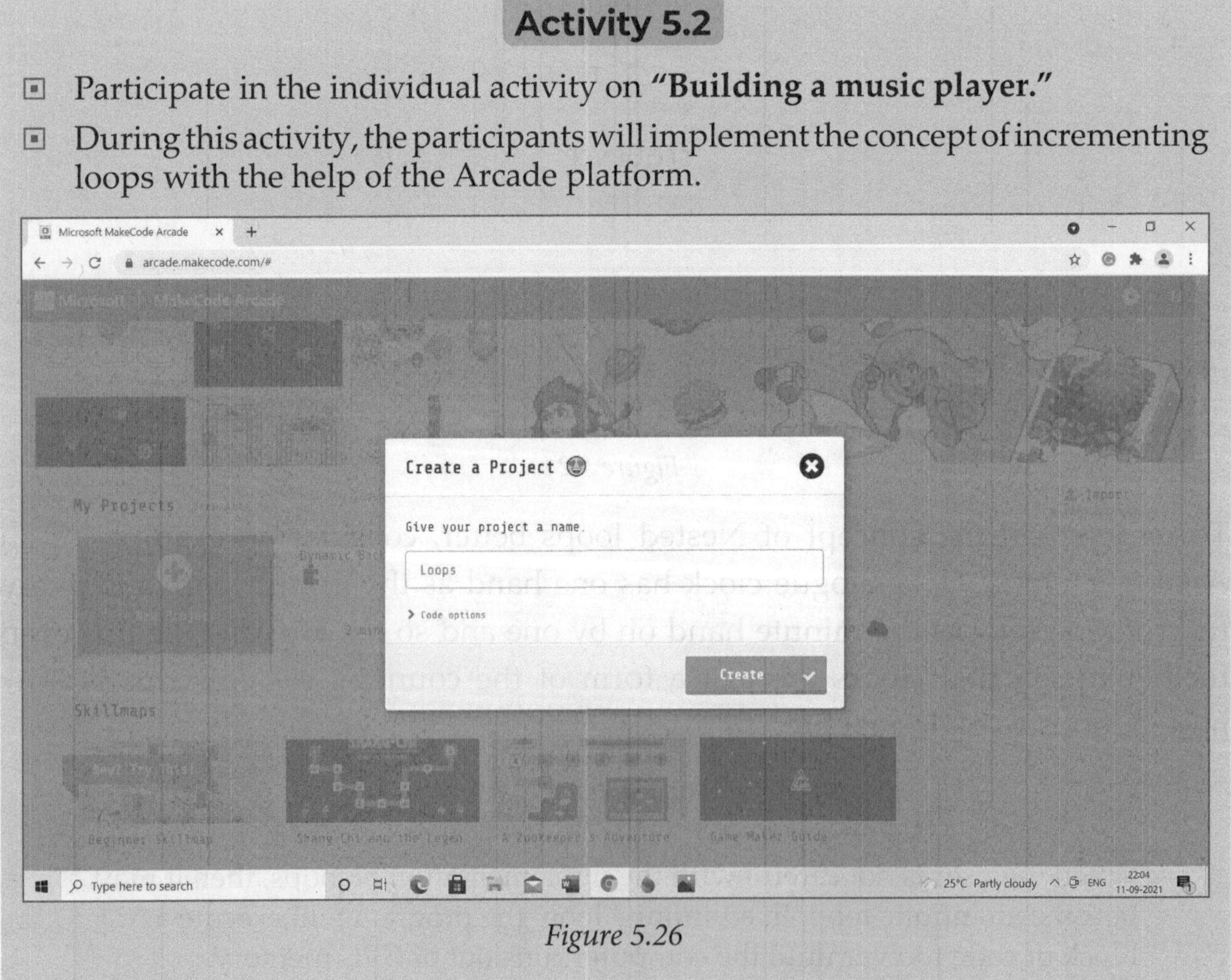

Figure 5.26

- The following steps are to be followed:

  Step 1: In the arcade MakeCode editor, click on the "Loops" link in the toolbox and then drag and drop the "on start" block to the play area.

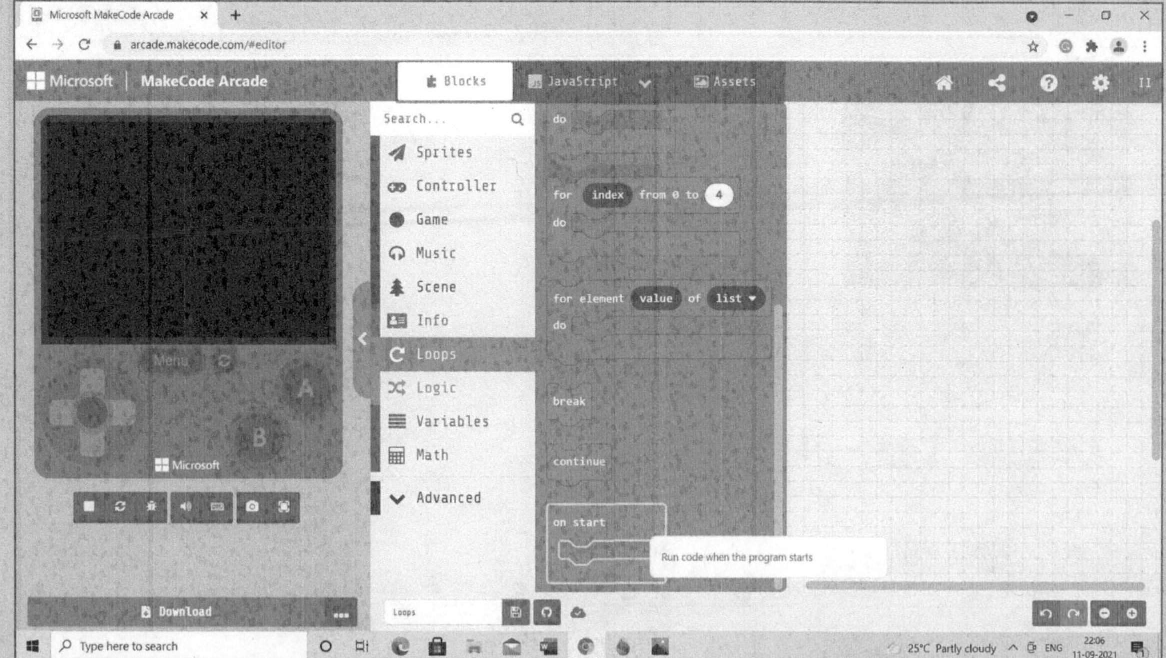

Figure 5.27

  Step 2: Again, click on the "Loops" link in the toolbox in the centre of the page. Drag and drop the "repeat 4 times do" block to the play area.

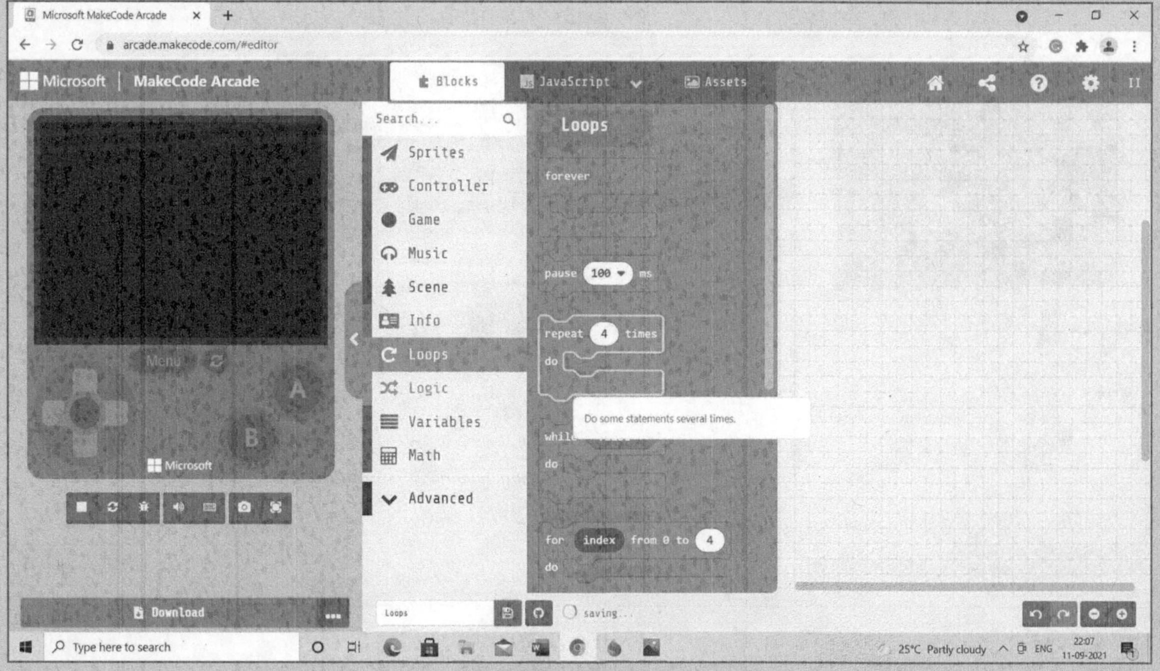

Figure 5. 28

Step 3: Now, move the other "repeat "block and place it inside the "start" block. Also, reset the value in the "repeat" block to "12".

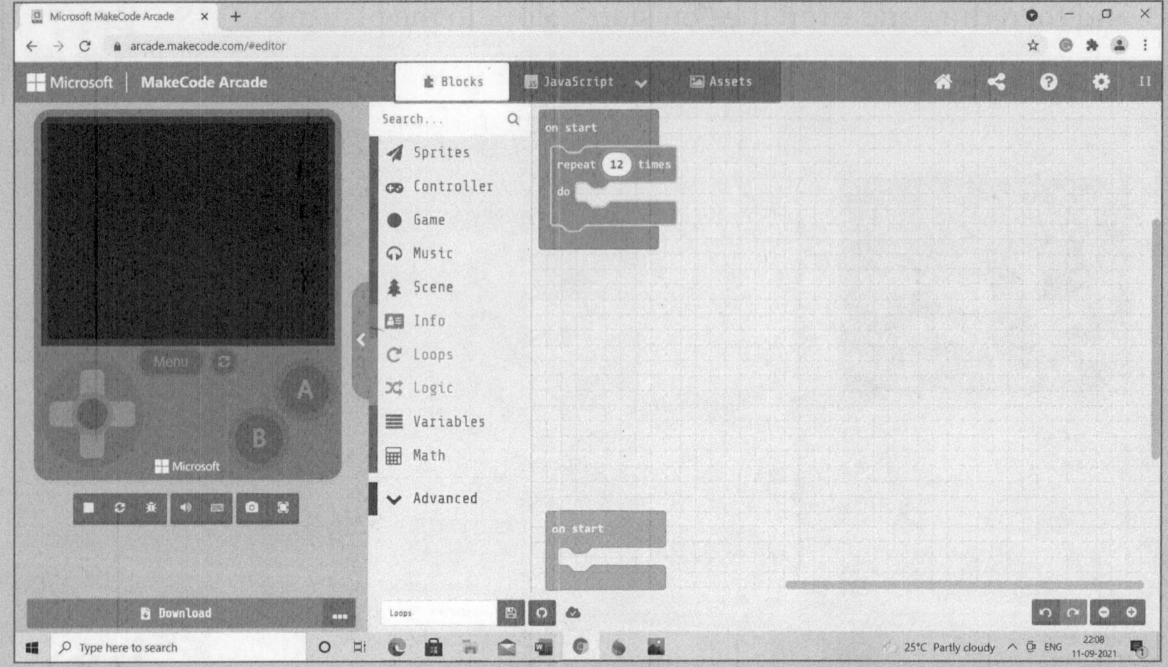

Figure 5. 29

Step 4: Click on the "Music" link from the toolbox and drag and drop the "play sound until done" block in the play area.

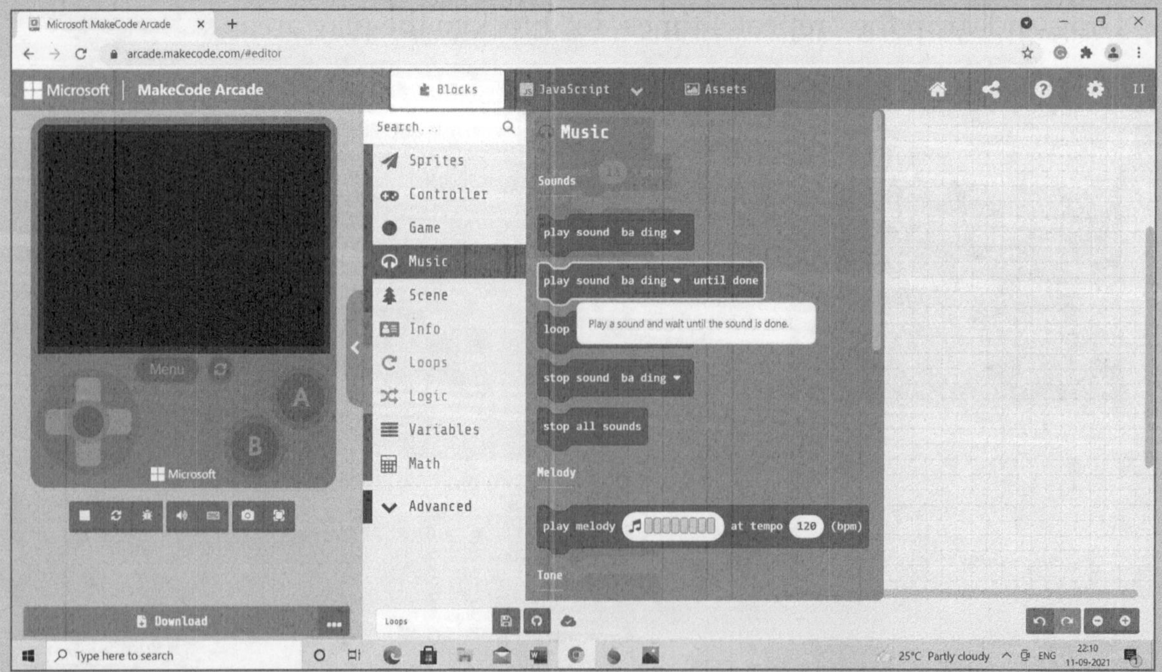

Figure 5.30

Step 5: Fix the "play sound until done" block in the "repeat" block.

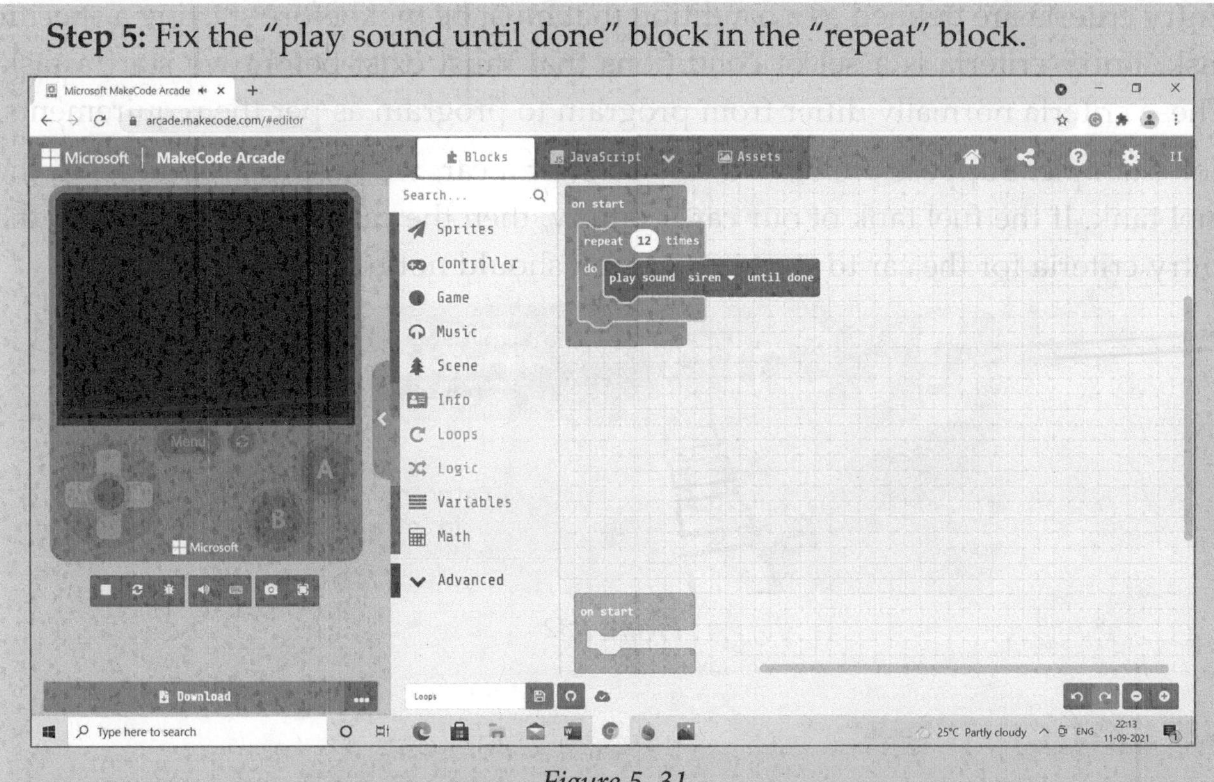

Figure 5. 31

- When we click on the play for the above exercise that we have created, we will hear the music 12 times. The loop repeats itself 12 times (counter that we had set). The flow starts with 1, and in each iteration, it increments once. Each time loop completes once iteration, and we will hear music once.

Factz Funda

The process of doing something again and again is called iteration. In computing, iteration is the technique of marking out a block of statements within a computer program for a defined number of repetitions.

5.4 ENTRY CRITERIA

As we have clearly understood the different types of loops and their iterations, it is also important to understand when and where one should start iterating through these loops. When the looping condition is true, then the code will enter a loop. It is important to define an entry criterion for the loop to ensure that the loop runs.

Entry criteria are defined as a condition that must be met before starting a specific task. Entry criteria is a set of conditions that must exist before we start a task. These criteria normally differ from program to program as per the requirements.

For example: Suppose we have a car. To start a car, we need petrol/diesel in the fuel tank. If the fuel tank of our car is empty, then the car won't start. Hence, the entry criteria for the car to start is fuel tank should not be empty.

Figure 5.32

5.5 EXIT CRITERIA

As discussed earlier, it is crucial to keep in mind that the looping condition should result in false at a certain point in time during coding/programming. Otherwise, the block of code will enter an infinite loop. Therefore, it is important to define an exit criterion for the loop to ensure that the loop does not enter an infinite loop.

Exit criteria is defined as a condition that must be met before completing a specified task. Exit criteria is a set of conditions that must exist before you can declare a program to be completed. It is an important component while defining a loop. Without an exit criterion, the program tends to enter in an infinite loop. Exit criteria differ from program to program as per the requirements.

Example: Suppose we have to write a code for printing numbers from 1 to 2000 using a loop. While creating a loop to print numbers from 1 to 2000, the exit criteria in that loop should exit the block of code when the 2000th number is printed; else, the program will enter an infinite loop.

5.6 BREAK STATEMENT

The break statement modifies the normal flow of execution while it terminates the existing loop and continues the execution of the statement following that loop. The break statement is required as sometimes the user wants to break out of a loop early when a condition is met.

Let us try to understand Break Statement with the help of pseudocode as given below:

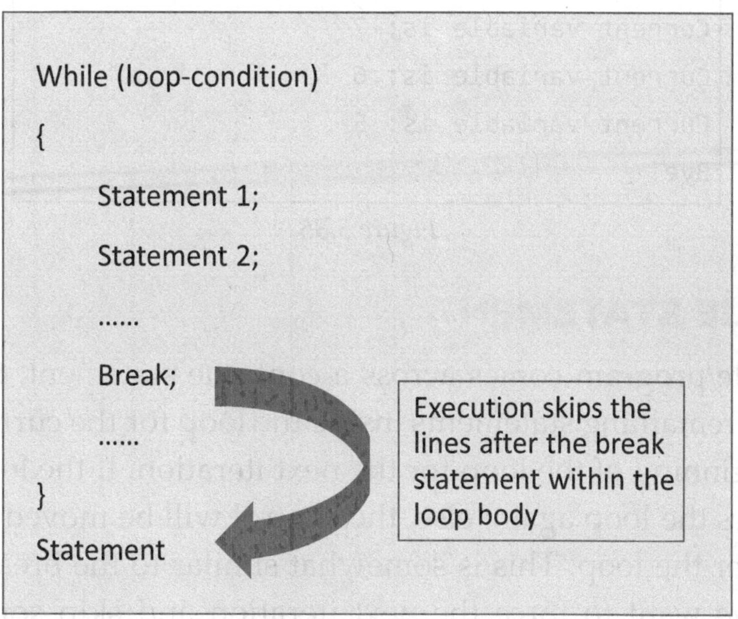

Figure 5.33

As we see, the control skips the lines after the break statement and executes the first statement outside the loop.

Example: Use break statement to print number from 10 to 4 and another print statement when you encounter break. The pseudo-code for this will look like below:

```
a = 10
while a > 0:
print 'Current variable is:', a
a = a -1
if a == 4:
    break
print "Bye!"
```

Figure 5.34

This is the result for the code:

```
Current variable is: 10
Current variable is: 9
Current variable is: 8
Current variable is: 7
Current variable is: 6
Current variable is: 5
Bye!
```

Figure 5.35

5.7 CONTINUE STATEMENT

Whenever a code/program comes across a continue statement, the control skips the execution of remaining statements inside the loop for the current iteration and jumps to the beginning of the loop for the next iteration. If the loop's condition is still true, it enters the loop again; else, the control will be moved to the statement immediately after the loop. This is somewhat similar to the break statement and is used when we want to force the next iteration and skip some lines of code within the loop.

Let us now understand continue statements with the below pseudocode:

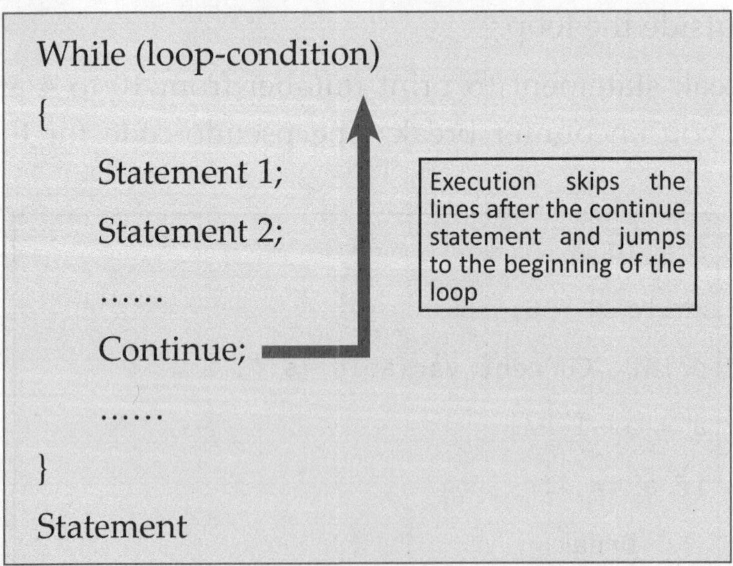

Figure 5.36

As we see, as soon as the continue statement is encountered, the lines below the continue statement are skipped. But unlike the break statement, the loop is not terminated. Instead, the control jumps to the beginning of the loop.

Example: Use 'continue' statement to print number from 9 to 0 and does not print when the value is 7.

The pseudo-code for this will look like below:

```
b = 9
while b > 0:
b = b -1
if b == 0:
    continue print 'Current variable is:', a
print "Welcome!"
```

Figure 5.37

This is the result of the code.

```
Current variable is: 9
Current variable is: 8
Current variable is: 6
Current variable is: 5
Current variable is: 4
Current variable is: 3
Current variable is: 2
Current variable is: 1
Current variable is: 0
Welcome!
```

Figure 5.38

A loop becomes an infinite loop when a condition never becomes false.

1. Which letter won't print while running the below pseudocode?

```
For letter in "coding":
        if letter == "o":
break
        print(letter)
print("End")
```

Figure 5.39

(a) 'd' (b) 'c' (c) 'i' (d) 'o'

2. An else statement should always be after an if statement which executes when the code is false.

(a) True (b) False

3. 'If' statement is used to execute some code when a statement is not true.

(a) True (b) False

4. A for loop executes for a specific number of times

(a) True (b) False

5. What is the name given to doing something over and over again or repeating code?

(a) Program (b) Code (c) Loop (d) Bug

6. When a break statement is encountered inside a loop, then the loop is immediately ended, and the program execution moves on to the next statement in the loop.

(a) True (b) False

7. What is the output of the below pseudocode?

```
count = 0;
sum = 0;
while (count<7)
{
   sum= sum + count;
   count= count +1
}
print sum;
```

Figure 5.40

(a) 0 (b) 2 (c) 5 (d) 7

8. Without a statement that eventually evaluates the while loop condition to false, the loop will continue indefinitely.

(a) True (b) False

9. A continue statement is used to skip all the remaining statements in the loop and moves the control back to the top of the loop.

(a) True (b) False

10. Which letter won't print while running the below pseudocode?

```
For letter in "coding":
        if letter == "i":
continue
        print(letter)
print("End")
```

Figure 5.41

(a) 'd' (b) 'c' (c) 'i' (d) 'o'

11. A while loop statement repeatedly executes a statement as long as the condition remains false.

(a) True (b) False

12. Which of the following symbols is the correct operator for equality testing?

(a) += (b) == (c) = (d) !

13. Loop is regarded as one of the basic logical structures of computer programming.

(a) True (b) False

14. Which of the following loops are called conditional loops?

(a) Nested loops (b) For loops

(c) While loops (d) All of the above

ANSWERS									
1. (a)	2. (a)	3. (b)	4. (a)	5. (c)	6. (a)	7. (d)	8. (a)	9. (a)	10. (c)
11. (b)	12. (b)	13. (a)	14. (c)						

SUMMARY

- A loop may be defined as a shape produced by a curve that bends round and crosses itself. Grammatically, loop means encircling.
- A loop may also be defined as a structure, series, or process, the end of which is connected to the beginning.
- Loop is regarded as one of the basic logical structures of computer programming.
- The need for defining the loop in a computer program is due to various reasons that is based on the tasks to be performed.
- In programming, repetition of a line or a block of code is also known as iteration.

- A loop is an algorithm which executes a block of code multiple times till the time a specified condition is met.
- A loop iterates a block of code multiple times till the time mentioned condition is satisfied.
- Iterator is an object which allows a programmer to traverse through all the elements of a collection, regardless of its specific implementation.
- We might tell the computer either to stop after it has repeated the loop a certain number of times or to stop once a certain condition is met.
- Loops provide the facility to execute a block of code repetitively, based on a condition and till the time a specified condition remains true.
- While programming, coder states the condition that should result false at a certain point of time to avoid its entry in an infinite loop.
- Execution of loops is based on iterations.
- To run a block of code in a loop, one needs to set a condition and set its number of iterations.
- Each time the condition is true, and the block of code executes once, it is counted to be one iteration.
- The range () function returns a sequence of numbers, starting from 0 by default, and increments by 1 (by default), and ends at a specified number.
- The loop will exit when the condition becomes false.
- Most loops have a variable which in programming terms is called counter variable.
- The counter variable keeps track of how many times the loop executed.
- A loop statement allows users to execute a statement or group of statements multiple times.
- 'While' Loops are also called 'conditional' loops.
- The 'While' loop can execute a set of commands till the condition is true.
- 'While' loops are those loops that will continue to go until a condition is no longer true.
- 'For' loops will repeat a block of code a set number of times as directed.
- The reason these loops are called 'for' loops is that we can tell our app how many times we want it to repeat to the code for.
- When there is a loop inside another loop, it is called a nested loop.
- In computing, iteration is the technique marking out of a block of statements within a computer program for a defined number of repetitions.
- Entry criteria is defined as a condition that must be met before starting a specific task.

- Exit criterion is a set of conditions that must exist before we can start a task.
- Exit criteria is defined as a condition that must be met before completing a specific task.
- Exit criterion is a set of conditions that must exist before you can declare a program to be completed.
- The break statement modifies the normal flow of execution while it terminates the existing loop and continues execution of the statement following that loop.
- A continue statement controls the execution of remaining statements inside the loop for the current iteration and jumps to the beginning of the loop for the next iteration.

PRACTICE TIME

(A) Fill in the blanks

1. A ____________ is defined as a shape produced by a curve that bends round and crosses itself. Grammatically, loop means encircling.
2. Execution of loops is based on ____________.
3. The ____________ () function returns a sequence of numbers, starting from 0 by default, and increments by 1 (by default), and ends at a specified number.
4. In programming, repetition of a line or a block of code is also known as ____________.
5. The loop will exit when the condition becomes ____________.
6. Each time the condition is true, and the block of code executes ____________, it is counted to be one iteration.
7. The ____________ variable keeps track of how many times the loop is executed.
8. ____________ criterion is defined as a condition that must be met before starting a specific task.
9. ____________ criterion is a set of conditions that must exist before we can start a task.
10. When there is a loop inside another loop, it is called a ____________ loop.

ANSWERS				
1. loop	2.iterations.	3. range	4. iteration	5. false
6. once	7.counter	8. Entry	9. Exit	10. nested

(B) True/ False type

1. A loop may also be defined as a structure, series, or process, the end of which is connected to the beginning.
2. Most loops do not have a counter variable.
3. A loop statement allows users to execute a statement or group of statements multiple times.
4. 'For' Loops are also called 'conditional' loops.
5. The 'While' loop can execute a set of commands till the condition is true.
6. 'Nested' loops will repeat a block of code a set number of times as directed.
7. A loop iterates a block of code multiple times till the time mentioned condition is satisfied.
8. Loops provide the facility to execute a block of code repetitively, based on a condition and till the time a specified condition remains true.
9. Iterator is an object which allows a programmer to traverse through all the elements of a collection, regardless of its specific implementation.
10. Exit criteria is defined as a condition that must be met before completing a specific task.

ANSWERS				
1. (T)	2. (F)	3. (T)	4. (F, while)	5. (T)
6. (F, For loops)	7. (T)	8. (T)	9. (T)	10. (T)

(C) Very Short Answers Questions

1. Define loops.
2. What do you mean by nested loops in programming?
3. What is an exit criterion?
4. What do you mean by iteration?
5. What is a break statement?
6. Define a continue statement.

(D) Short Answer Questions

1. How do we increment loops?
2. What is the reason they are called 'for' loops?
3. What do you mean by iterator and nested loops?

(E) High Order Thinking Skill Questions (HOTS)

1. Why are while loops called conditional loops?
2. Using the Arcade MakeCode platform, create an example for nested loops.

(F) Project

Write a program using loops that ask the user to enter an even number. If the number entered does not display an appropriate message and asks them to enter a number again. Do not stop until an even number is entered. Print a congratulations message at the end.

REFERENCES

- https://www.acm.org/code-of-ethics
- https://arcade.makecode.com
- https://minecraft.makecode.com
- https://education.minecraft.net/class-resources/computer-science-subject-kit
- https://education.minecraft.net/class-resources/computer-science-subjectkit ACM, Inc. 2021.
- https://education.minecraft.net/hour-of-code 202
- https://www.codingal.com
- https://www.idtech.com/blog/coding-terminology-list
- https://www.codewizardshq.com/kids-guide-200-common-programming-terms/

Annexure 1
Coding Terminology

Abstraction: A simplified representation of something more complex.

Accessibility: The design of products, devices, services, or environments taking into consideration the ability for all users to access, including people who experience disabilities or those who are limited by older or slower technology.

Algorithm: A set of instructions that are followed to solve a problem.

Arithmetic operators: Operators that are essential in almost every application, especially in games.

Assignment operators: Operators that combine variable assignments with arithmetic operators.

Augmented reality (AR): An interactive experience where digital objects are placed in a real-world environment in real time.

Binary alphabet: The two options used in your binary code.

Binary numbers: A computer's way to represent information using only 1's and 0's.

Bit: The individual 1's and 0's in binary are called bits.

Block-based programming language: Any programming language that lets users create programs by manipulating "blocks" or graphical programming elements, rather than writing code using text.

Blockly: The visual programming language used in Code.org's online learning system for K-5 students.

Bug: An error in a program that prevents the program from running as expected.

Byte: The most common fundamental unit of digital data. A single byte is 8 bits-worth of data.

C++: A low-level versatile programming language.

Camel case: A system in which the first word of the name of a variable is lowercase and each new word after that is capitalized.

Code: The language that programmers create and use to tell a computer what to do.

Coding languages: Languages that computer can understand.

Coding: A set of instructions for computers to follow to complete a task.

Command: An instruction for the computer. Many commands put together make up algorithms and computer programs.

Computational thinking: Modifying a problem in such a way that it can be modeled or solved using a computer or machine.

Computer program: A group of instructions given to a computer to be processed.

Conditional statements: Statements that evaluate to true or false.

Conditionals: Statements that only run under certain conditions.

Crowdsourcing: Getting help from a large group of people to finish something faster.

Cyberbullying: Doing something on the internet, usually again and again, to make another personal feel angry, sad, or scared.

Data: Information. Often, quantities, characters, or symbols that are the inputs and outputs of computer programs.

Debugging: Finding and fixing problems in an algorithm or program.

Decompose: Break a problem down into smaller pieces.

Digital citizen: Someone who acts safely, responsibly, and respectfully online.

Digital footprint: The information about someone on the Internet.

Double-click: Press the mouse button very quickly two times.

Drag: Click the mouse button and hold as the user move the mouse pointer to a new location.

Drop: Release the mouse button to "let go" of an item that the user was dragging.

Else statements: The statements are used to do something else when the condition in the if statement isn't true.

For loops: Loops that allow you to run a block of code repeatedly to run a block of code for a set number of times.

Function call: The piece of code that you add to a program to indicate that the program should run the code inside a function at a certain time.

Function: A block of code that can be referenced by name to run the code it contains.

If statement: A statement that runs a block of code based on whether or not a condition is true.

Input: A way to give information to a computer.

Integrated Development Environment: A software where you type your code and run your programs for making coding simpler.

Internet: A group of computers and servers that are connected to each other.

IP address: A number assigned to any item that is connected to the Internet.

Iteration: A repetitive action or command typically created with programming loops.

Java: A powerful multi-platform programming language.

Linux: An open-source operating system designed to run on multiple types of devices, like laptops, phones, tablets, robots, and many others.

Loop: The action of doing something over and over again.

Online: Connected to the Internet.

Output: A way to get information out of a computer.

Packets: Small chunks of information that have been carefully formed from larger chunks of information.

Parameter: An extra piece of information passed to a function to customize it for a specific need.

Pattern matching: Finding similarities between things.

Pixel: Short for "picture element", the fundamental unit of a digital image, typically a tiny square or dot that contains a single point of colour of a larger image.

Program: An algorithm that has been coded into something that can be run by a machine.

Programming: The art of creating a program.

Run program: Cause the computer to execute the commands you've written in your program.

Search engine: A program that searches for and identifies items in a database that correspond to keywords or characters specified by the user, used especially for finding particular sites on the World Wide Web.

Servers: Computers that exist only to provide things to others.

Toolbox: The tall grey bar in the middle section of any online learning system that contains all of the commands the user can use to write the program.

URL (universal resource locator): An easy-to-remember address for calling a web page .

Username: A name you make up so that you can see or do things on a website, sometimes called a "screen name."

Variable: A placeholder for a piece of information that can change.

Virtual **Reality:** An interactive experience where digital objects creates a completely artificial environment

Website: A collection of interlinked web pages on the World Wide Web.

While loop: A loop that continues to repeat while a condition is true.

Wi-Fi: A wireless method of sending information using radio waves.

Workspace: The white area on the right side of any online learning system where the user drag and drop commands to build the program.

Annexure 2
Some Famous Coders

Alan Cooper,
Developer of Visual Basics

Alan Kay,
Developer OOP (Object-Oriented Programming)

Bjarne Stroustrup,
Developer of C++

Brendan Eich,
Developer of Java Script

Guido van Rossum,
Creator of Python Language

John Backus,
Inventor of Fortran

James Gosling,
Developer of Java

Robin Milner,
Inventor of Machine Learning

References (Pictures/Photographs/Figures)

1.1 https://lifelearners.ng/the-underrated-benefits-of-learning-to-code/

1.2 https://www.nowwireless.com/traffic-lights

1.3 http://blogs.egusd.net/1computerlab/

1.4 https://www.ernestdempsey.com/what-programming-skills-and-languages-are-needed-in-2016/

1.5 https://miro.medium.com/max/3840/1*J4Lkof6K3jZpKrxVXdy-lw.jpeg

1.9 https://www.thewowstyle.com/how-can-smart-technology-ensure-safer-construction-sites/

2.1 https://blog.eduonix.com/internet-of-things/6-machine-learning-algorithms-learn-newbie/

2.2 https://www.indiatoday.in/education-today/featurephilia/story/tips-to-learn-coding-for-beginners-of-every-age-complete-guide-to-coding-tips-1745823-2020-12-01

2.3 https://tiki.vn/oxford-basic-english-dictionary-4th-edition-p368503.html

2.7 https://thegadgetflow.com/portfolio/wireless-coding-blocks/

2.8 https://www.researchgate.net/figure/Example-of-coding-in-the-block-coding-platform-Scratch_fig2_331260198

2.9 https://developers.google.com/blockly

2.10 https://www.computerhope.com/cdn/jacquard-loom.gif

3.1 https://www.techworm.net/2017/02/microsofts-ai-deepcoder-learns-coding-stealing-others.html

3.2 https://sites.google.com/a/tdsb.on.ca/coding-in-the-elementary-grades/programming-concepts/variables

4.1 https://blog.uk.fujitsu.com/digital-transformation/tackling-the-ai-data-challenge-could-synthetic-data-be-the-answer/attachment/binary-code-transforming-ai-robot-face/#.YfLxY-pByp4

5.1 https://morioh.com/p/2e5867121898

5.2 https://www.shutterstock.com/video/search/amusement?missingAssetId=62365

5.3 https://www.chronicle.com/article/the-holy-grail-of-class-discussion/

5.32 https://i0.wp.com/www.thinksys.com/wp-content/uploads/2017/01/entry-exit-criteria.png?resize=848%2C307&ssl=1